"*Faithful in Christ* goes to the core of priestly identity and touches upon some of the most significant areas involved in its ongoing renewal. One of its underlying themes deals with the importance of spiritual formation as the unifying principle of priestly life and ministry. Another is the way a priest's personal relationship with Christ affects the manner in which he lives and conducts his priestly ministry. Still another is the integrating function of priestly ministry with priestly life. Although the 'Year for Priests' is now behind us, my hope is that this collection of lectures will keep alive the spirit behind it.

'The priesthood,' Saint John Vianney tells us, 'is the love of the heart of Jesus.' This book is all about the love of the heart of the priest in his efforts to make the love of Jesus palpably present to the people he serves."

+ His Eminence Cardinal Justin Rigali
Archbishop of Philadelphia
From the Foreword

"*Faithful in Christ: The Ministry and Life of the Catholic Priest* is a welcome and insightful addition to the body of recent literature which presents the truth about the Catholic Priesthood. These lectures, presented originally in 2010 to commemorate 'The Year for Priests,' are a timeless reminder of just who the priest really is in every year, in every place—a son of the Father, chosen to stand in the person of the Son Jesus Christ by the power of the Holy Spirit, for the salvation of the world.

With both a personal knowledge of and deep respect for all of the priest contributors to this volume, I can offer no greater endorsement of their work than to say that they are themselves witnesses to the very priesthood about which they have written. Their treatment of the pillars upon which are built an authentic priestly life and ministry can only deepen the reader's love for Christ and his priests.

No doubt, priests will find in these presentations, together with the reflection questions and suggested readings, a fruitful source for discussion, study and prayer. All the faithful and the community at large will find here a window into the enriching and inspiring reality of the Catholic priesthood and of what is behind, or better, within, the men who daily strive to live as 'Holy Priests for a Holy People.'"

+ Most Rev. Daniel E. Thomas
Auxiliary Bishop of Philadelphia

"At a time when many eyes are fixed upon the ugliness of priestly scandal, eyes of faith submit anew to the ever-soft light of grace, which illumines an undiminished beauty of priestly ministry and life, willed by Jesus, shared with men, bringing life to the world. The present work, the fruit of a conference at St. Charles Borromeo Seminary during the 'Year for Priests,' ably presents the priesthood needed for our age and for every age. It is a timely glimpse of a timeless call that is lived in time."

Rev. Shaun L. Mahoney, S.T.D.
Rector, St. Charles Borromeo Seminary

FAITHFUL IN CHRIST
The Ministry and Life of the Catholic Priest

FAITHFUL IN CHRIST

The Ministry and Life of the Catholic Priest

Edited by

Dennis J. Billy, C.Ss.R.

LEONINE PUBLISHERS
PHOENIX, ARIZONA

Nihil Obstat: Reverend Joseph T. Shenosky, S.T.D.
                  Censor Librorum
                  Philadelphiae, 2-14-11

Imprimatur: ✠ Cardinal Justin Rigali
                  Archiepiscopus Philadelphiensis
                  Philadelphiae, 2-14-11

Published by Leonine Publishers LLC
P.O. Box 8099
Phoenix, Arizona 85066

ISBN-13: 978-0-9836740-1-6

Library of Congress Control Number: 2011932060

10 9 8 7 6 5 4 3 2 1

Printed in the United States of America

Cover image: "Chartres Saint-Aignan96," by Reinhardhauke, licensed under the Creative Commons Attribution-Share Alike 3.0 Unported license.

Visit us online at www.leoninepublishers.com
For more information: info@leoninepublishers.com

In honor of

Saint Jean-Baptiste-Marie Vianney
Curé of Ars,
Patron Saint of Priests

*The priesthood is the love
of the heart of Christ.*

—The Curé of Ars

CONTENTS

ACKNOWLEDGMENTS

Unless otherwise stated, all quotations from Sacred Scripture come from the *New American Bible* (Washington, D.C.: Confraternity of Christian Doctrine, 1970, 1986, 1991), available on the Vatican website at http://www.vatican.va/archive/ENG0839/_INDEX.HTM.

Unless otherwise stated, all quotations from Catholic magisterial documents come from the Vatican website at http://www.vatican.va/phome_en.htm.

The Epilogue was previously published in *The Priest* (61, no. 11, 2005: 14). During the "Year for Priests," it was the text for a photo display on the priesthood that was arranged by Mrs. Ene Andrilli for St. Charles Borromeo Seminary's Ryan Memorial Library.

FOREWORD

+ *Cardinal Justin Rigali*

On June 19, 2009, on the Solemnity of the Most Sacred Heart of Jesus, Pope Benedict XVI proclaimed a "Year for Priests" in commemoration of the 150th anniversary of the death of Saint John Vianney.

In his letter proclaiming this event, the Holy Father stated that the purpose of this year was "to deepen the commitment of all priests to interior renewal for the sake of a more forceful and incisive witness to the Gospel in today's world." As part of its official celebration, the Archdiocese of Philadelphia organized a lecture series on the priesthood entitled, "Faithful in Christ: The Ministry and Life of the Catholic Priest." The lectures were offered during Lent of 2010 and were accomplished through the auspices of the John Cardinal Krol Chair of Moral Theology, an endowed professorship at Saint Charles Borromeo Seminary in Overbrook, one of the oldest Roman Catholic Seminaries in the United States.

The lecture series was open to the public and celebrated the gift of the priesthood to the people of God by looking at various facets of a priest's ministry and life: his life of prayer and worship, his study and proclamation of Sacred Scripture, his understanding and implementation of Church teaching, his exercise of compassion and forgiveness, his qualities of pastoral service, and his exercise of leadership in the Church community. The presenters were all high-ranking members of the seminary faculty with doctoral degrees from pontifical universities in Rome or the United States. An added benefit of these lectures was that they afforded members of the seminary faculty an opportunity to share their reflections on the Catholic priesthood with a wider audience. Now collected in book form, the potential for broad distribution of their ideas is even greater.

It gives me great pleasure to write the foreword for this book. The topics it covers go to the core of priestly identity and touch upon some of the most significant areas involved in its ongoing renewal. One of its underlying themes deals with the importance of spiritual formation as the unifying principle of priestly life and ministry. Another is the way a priest's personal relationship with Christ affects the manner in which he lives and conducts his priestly ministry. Still another is the integrating function of priestly ministry with priestly life. Although the "Year for Priests" is now behind us, my hope is that this collection of lectures will keep alive the spirit behind it.

"The priesthood," Saint John Vianney tells us, "is the love of the heart of Jesus." This book is all about the love of the heart of the priest in his efforts to make the love of Jesus palpably present to the people he serves.

*+ **Cardinal Justin Rigali***
Archbishop of Philadelphia

INTRODUCTION

Rev. Msgr. Joseph G. Prior, S.T.D.

Chapter five of the Letter to the Hebrews opens, "Every high priest is taken from among men and made their representative before God, to offer gifts and sacrifices for sins" (Heb 5:1). Jesus, the great High Priest, represents man before God and offers the one perfect sacrifice for the atonement of sin; He offers Himself. Priests share in the one priesthood of Jesus Christ—in their ministry and through their lives. Like Christ, the priest is called to lay down his life for his friends: the faithful whom he serves.

When Pope Benedict XVI inaugurated the "Year for Priests" to commemorate the one hundred fiftieth anniversary of the death of Saint John Vianney, patron of priests, the Holy Father expressed his hopes that this year would be a time of renewal in the priesthood, whereby priests deepen their relationship with the One High Priest. Thus, their sanctity is renewed and strengthened for faithful service to the Gospel. In his letter proclaiming the "Year for Priests," the Holy Father encouraged priests to deepen their commitment "to interior renewal for the sake of a more forceful and incisive witness to the Gospel in today's world."[1]

To foster this renewal, Saint Charles Borromeo Seminary sponsored a series of public lectures by faculty members in Lent 2010 in observance of the "Year for Priests." The series was organized by Dennis J. Billy, C.Ss.R., the holder of the John Cardinal Krol Chair of Moral Theology. It was part of the larger celebration of the "Year

---

[1] "Letter of His Holiness Pope Benedict XVI Proclaiming a Year for Priests on the 150th Anniversary of the *Dies Natalis* of the Curé of Ars," accessed May 7, 2010, http://www.vatican.va/holy_father/benedict_ xvi/letters/2009/documents/hf_ben-xvi_let_20090616_anno-sacerdotale_ en.html.

for Priests" in the Archdiocese of Philadelphia, the theme of which was "Holy Priest for a Holy People." Priests in the Archdiocese and neighboring dioceses, along with all interested persons, were invited to attend. Through the publication of these lectures we hope to celebrate the ministry and life of priests with the wider public.

This lecture series is now available in book form: *Faithful in Christ: The Ministry and Life of the Catholic Priest*. Its title underscores an essential point about Catholic belief and practice: Faith in and faithfulness to Jesus Christ are hallmarks of holiness. In the priesthood, as in all aspects of the faith, Jesus is central; in Him, the life and ministry of priests are intimately united. The faithfulness of priests strengthens and grows through an ever-deeper relationship with Jesus, which enables them to proclaim His Word ever more effectively.

There is an intimate connection between the ministry and life of the priest. The ministry of the priest in service to the Word of God in all its manifestations flows from the life he lives as one ordained in the priesthood of Jesus Christ.

This book builds on the official Catholic teaching on the male priesthood[2] by exploring some of the most fundamental dimensions of the ministry and life of priests. It stresses the importance of priests being men of prayer, men of the Word, men who communicate sound doctrine, men of compassion, men of service, and men of vision and leadership. Its purpose is to provide an in-depth examination of the vocation to the priesthood by looking at these important dimensions of priestly life in detail.

To guide its reflections, the book makes frequent use of recent magisterial teaching on the priesthood. In his 1992 Post-Synodal Exhortation, *Pastores dabo vobis*, arguably the most important ecclesial statement on priestly formation since the Second Vatican Council, Pope John Paul II describes four essential areas of formation in the development of the future priest: the human, spiritual, intellectual, and pastoral. Pope Benedict XVI describes this process of formation in terms of cooperation, allowing the Lord to shape and mold the seminarian into the person and priest he is called to be. This process affects all aspects of the seminarian's life. At the heart of

---

[2] John Paul II, Apostolic Letter, *Ordinatio Sacerdotalis*, no. 4.

this process is spiritual formation and growth in holiness. As Pope John Paul II notes:

> ... just as for all the faithful spiritual formation is central and unifies their being and living as Christians, that is, as new creatures in Christ who walk in the Spirit, so too for every priest his spiritual formation is the core which unifies and gives life to his being a priest and his acting as a priest.[3]

This unifying aspect of spiritual formation is further specified in the *Program for Priestly Formation*, which are the directives guiding the work of priestly formation in the United States:

> Since spiritual formation is the core that unifies the life of a priest, it stands at the heart of seminary life and is the center around which all other aspects are integrated. Human, intellectual, and pastoral formation are indispensable in developing the seminarian's relationship and communion with God and his ability to communicate God's truth and love to others in the likeness of Jesus Christ, the Good Shepherd and eternal High Priest.[4]

This book's six chapters underscore the central, integrating role of spiritual formation in the life and ministry of priests.

In "Men of Prayer: Priests and Holiness" (Chapter One), Msgr. Michael K. Magee reminds us that the call to holiness requires the priest "to be the icon of Christ *both Crucified and Risen*." The priest is someone who both surrenders himself to the service of the Lord and puts himself forward to claim the world for Christ in the here and now. Priests embrace the dying of Christ, so the power of the Risen Christ may be manifest in their lives and in the life of the Church.

In "Men of the Word: Priests and Scripture" (Chapter Two), Father Patrick J. Brady discusses the responsibility priests have to proclaim the Good News of Jesus Christ through a meditative reading and careful study of the revealed texts. Preaching God's Word is one of the priest's most sacred responsibilities, one that requires great prayer and dedication. God's Word gives meaning, purpose, and direction to a priest's life and lies at the very heart of his ministry.

---

[3] John Paul II, *Pastores Dabo Vobis*, no. 45.

[4] *Program for Priestly Formation*, no. 115.

In "Men of Faith: Priests and Church Teaching" (Chapter Three), Father Robert A. Pesarchick tells us that in the Church there is not only a hierarchy of truths but also a hierarchy of authoritative teaching. Priests must have an accurate knowledge of these distinctions and make frequent use of them when they instruct the faithful in matters regarding faith and morals.

In "Men of Compassion: Priests and Forgiveness" (Chapter Four), Father Dennis J. Billy, C.Ss.R., claims that priests are called to be men of compassion because they seek to follow in the footsteps of Christ. Using the parable of the Good Samaritan as his point of departure, he identifies practical ways in which priests can become the compassionate and forgiving men they are called to be.

In "Men of Service: Priests and the Pastoral Life" (Chapter Five), Father Anthony J. Costa tells us that priests are called to wash the feet of others as Christ did by giving themselves in humble service to others. They do so by being rooted in Christ through lives that are centered on the Eucharist, imbued with prayer, motivated by pastoral charity, inspired by Christ's emptying of self, and led by an eagerness to continually discern God's will.

In "Men of Vision: Priests and Leadership" (Chapter Six), Msgr. David E. Diamond outlines the major models of leadership theory and identifies three with the most significance for priests: the transformational, moral, and servant models. The servant model, he maintains, is especially significant for priests, since it places them in the long line of prophets culminating in Christ who call their people to an ongoing fidelity to God's Word.

To help the reader delve more deeply into the topics discussed, each of these chapters is supplemented by a series of reflection questions and suggestions for further reading. The book ends with an epilogue on the priesthood ("A Priest Is"), which offers the reader a synthetic presentation of the priesthood in its human, spiritual, intellectual, and pastoral dimensions.

The priesthood is a great gift to the Church and helps us to experience the love and mercy of God in the life of the Church. The *Catechism of the Catholic Church* describes this as follows:

> The ordained ministry or ministerial priesthood is at the service of the baptismal priesthood. The ordained priesthood guarantees that it really is Christ who acts in

the sacraments through the Holy Spirit for the Church. The saving mission entrusted by the Father to his incarnate Son was committed to the apostles and through them to their successors: they receive the Spirit of Jesus to act in his name and in his person. The ordained minister is the sacramental bond that ties the liturgical action to what the apostles said and did and, through them, to the words and actions of Christ, the source and foundation of the sacraments.[5]

It is our hope that those who read this text—priests, religious, or laity—will come to a deeper appreciation of the great gift of priesthood, the corresponding responsibilities of the priest, and of the need for continued interior renewal of the priesthood. Along with a deeper appreciation, we hope that those who read this book will be inspired to pray for priests and an increase in priestly vocations for the Church.

In conclusion, I would like to express the gratitude of the entire Saint Charles Borromeo Seminary community to His Eminence Justin Cardinal Rigali, Archbishop of Philadelphia, for his support of this work and all the efforts of Saint Charles Borromeo Seminary. We are also grateful for his foreword to this volume. Particular thanks is expressed to Father Dennis J. Billy, C.Ss.R., the John Cardinal Krol Chair of Moral Theology at Saint Charles Borromeo Seminary, for organizing the lecture series and serving as editor of this book. Thanks to all the presenters for their research, writing, and presentation of their lectures, to all those involved with the preparation for the lecture series which was a great success, to all those who attended the lecture series, and to those who will reap the benefits of the series through its book form.

---

[5] *CCC*, no. 1120.

Chapter One

MEN OF PRAYER:
PRIESTS AND HOLINESS

Rev. Msgr. Michael K. Magee, S.T.D.

In one sense, it is exhilarating to reflect on the theme of holiness in relation to the priesthood. For most of us who are priests now, or who are currently in priestly formation, we know it was some manifestation of the holiness of the priesthood that first attracted us to this life by its mysterious magnetism. For all of us who are baptized, we know that it is through the mediation of Christ's priesthood that we received those holy things that we treasure most in this life: the forgiveness of sins; the Holy Eucharist; the preaching of God's Word; blessings on ourselves, our activities, and our articles of devotion; the pastoral leadership of our parish and diocesan communities; and the healing power of the oil of the sick. Even if we have never reflected deeply on what the word "holiness" might mean, we are profoundly aware of the fact that these particular gifts are those that we could have never given ourselves or earned through any amount of effort, because their origin lies in a world beyond the limitations of our own. Yet, somehow the ministry of the priest either transported us into that world, or made that world present to us here on earth.

At the same time, *especially* for those of us who are priests or in priestly formation, the theme of "Priests and Holiness" is a daunting one: most of all, I dare say, for the one who was asked to prepare this reflection. It is one thing to be asked to expound upon one's area of expertise, but how could anyone really claim "holiness" as an area of expertise? And without being able to claim the expertise, how is it possible even to describe holiness or to suggest how it might be recognized? Certainly the only way to begin is by looking to the Sacred Scriptures and to the Church's Tradition.

WHAT IS "HOLINESS"?

Our understanding of holiness in the Latin ecclesial tradition is formed from the Latin word *sanctitas* in the Vulgate version of the Bible. This word renders two distinct Greek verbs: *hagios*, which connotes that which is "separate," belonging to the sphere of the "totally other" and therefore inspiring awe; and *hosios*, which expresses the sanction of the divine will or law.[1] The Hebrew word *qadosh*—used, for example, in the "Holy! Holy! Holy [is the] LORD God of hosts" exclaimed by the seraphim in Isaiah 6—likewise comes from an original root meaning "separation" or "apartness."[2] Here we can see why it is so difficult to establish a clear criterion for ascertaining the presence of true holiness. Precisely because holiness pertains to a world other than that of our immediate experience, we lack any internal compass that would enable us to verify its authenticity. Holiness is holiness precisely because it pertains to the realm of God rather than the realm of our ordinary existence.

If we follow Dante's *Divine Comedy* to the very depths of hell in his *Inferno*, we find there an image that is rather disturbing in its implications for the human search for God. Dante describes his shock when he finally encounters the lord of the netherworld: *Oh quanto parve a me gran maraviglia quand'io vidi tre facce a la sua testa!*—translated by Longfellow to say, "Oh what a marvel it

---

[1] Cf. H. Pope, "Holiness," *Catholic Encyclopedia* (New York: Robert Appleton Company, 1910), accessed February 12, 2010, http://www.newadvent.org/cathen/07386a.htm. Despite the existence now of a *New Catholic Encyclopedia* of much more recent publication, citations here are given from this 1910 edition not only because of its greater accessibility due to online publication, but also because its various articles, of high scholarly value, remain entirely adequate today for the specific terms treated in this paper.

[2] Francis Brown, *The New Brown-Driver-Briggs-Gesenius Hebrew and English Lexicon* (Peabody, MA: Hendrickson, 1979), 871.

appeared to   me / when I beheld three faces on his head!"[3] Dante's insight of the devil as a parody of the triune God rings true in its implication that the forces in this world most vigorously opposed to God may in fact be presenting to people a false image of holiness, and leading them astray in precisely this way.

If we are mistaken about who God is and what He wants, and left only with the knowledge that the holy is identified as the totally other with respect to our own experience, there is then nothing to prevent us from identifying as holiness anything that is simply eccentric. In fact, most of us can remember some example of just such a spectacle. Under the same conditions, there is not necessarily anything to prevent our characterizing even unspeakable cruelty as holy. In our own day, we toppled buildings and bereaved families to testify to that fact: terrible scars left on our world in misguided homage to a counterfeit of holiness.

Holiness is only made possible, then, by means of true self-disclosure of God's own interiority, reliably ascertainable by human beings, and able even to be imitated by them in some way. Only when God accommodates Himself to human reason and human perception, can the human person be elevated beyond his native powers. He is then raised to a life that transcends the physical and moral limitations of this passing world. The Letter to the Ephesians (4:22-24) describes that transformation now made possible by the coming of God as Man: "Put away the old man living according to your former way of life, corrupted by deceitful urges; instead, be renewed in the spirit of your minds, and put on the new man created in God's way in righteousness and the holiness of truth."[4]

This passage from the Epistle tells us several things, then, about the pursuit of holiness. First, holiness necessarily requires a letting go of something in order to take hold of something else. Second, since the pattern of holiness exists outside of ourselves, holiness is not something that can be achieved by us; rather, it can only be *received*. And finally, as we have already noted, the pattern for holiness of life is not something that can be conceived by us on the basis of merely

---

[3] Dante Alighieri, *Inferno,* Canto XXXIV, accessed February 13, 2010, http://dante.ilt.columbia.edu/new/comedy/index.html.

[4] The English translations of Sacred Scripture in this chapter are those of the author.

human experience, but can be found only in the authenticated revelation of God's own life. We find that authenticated revelation in the Sacred Scriptures and in the life of Christ mediated to us also through the Church. Since it is found there, let us now undertake a survey of these sources in search of a reliable pattern of what it means to come into contact with God's holiness and to pursue it in our own lives—first as men, and then specifically as priests.

FEAR OF THE HOLY

A number of the stories of the Old Testament exemplify a strange paradox in the pursuit of holiness. Although it is impossible for anyone to pursue holiness without first encountering the living God, that very encounter with God, when we see it narrated in the Scriptures, seems first of all to fill the human person with trepidation. We are told, for example, that when Moses encountered the LORD in the burning bush, he "hid his face, for he was afraid to look at God" (Ex 3:6). In fact, later, even after Moses became intimate with God and courageous enough to want to see God's glory, God Himself reminds him, "my face you cannot see, for no man sees me and still lives" (Ex 33:20).

Time and time again in the Sacred Scriptures, a true encounter with the All-Holy God seems to fill His servants with the sense of their own inadequacy and sinfulness, especially in the face of what God clearly asks of them. When called by God to lead the children of Israel out of slavery, Moses objects, "Who am I that I should go to Pharaoh and lead the Israelites out of Egypt?" (Ex 3:11). And later, in the same way, Gideon, when he is told by God that he is to save Israel from the hand of Midian, he too is overcome with a sense of his own smallness: "Please, my Lord, how can I save Israel? My family is the meanest in Manasseh, and I am the most insignificant in my father's house" (Jgs 6:14). Then Isaiah beheld the vision of the Lord sitting on His lofty throne in the Temple, surrounded by the seraphim who were veiling their faces before His holiness. Isaiah's reaction is similar: "Woe is me, I am doomed! For I am a man of unclean lips, living among a people of unclean lips; yet my eyes have seen the King, the LORD of hosts!" (Is 6:5).

Then, at the boundary between the two Testaments, in the last and the greatest of the Prophets, we see the same melting away of the self in the presence of the Holy One, but now the fear has given way to a joyful yielding of self. John the Baptist *has* seen the face of God, and he *does* die. But his death is one that prepares the way for the Lord. In fact, his death does not occur only when his head is severed and brought to Herod by the soldiers. It occurs first by an interior decision expressed in the words that he says to his disciples: "He must increase; I must decrease" (Jn 3:30). Parallel to those famous passages in the Gospel of John in which Jesus speaks the words *ego eimi*—"I am"—as a majestic act of self-disclosure, there is another series of statements in which John the Baptist, faced with those who mistake him for the Messiah, utters the negation "I am not" (1:20-21, 27; 3:28). It was those words of John the Baptist, more than his decapitation, that showed forth most clearly the continuing validity in the New Testament of the Old Testament maxim that anyone who saw the face of God would have to die. And it was John's own attitude that showed us that there is more than one way to die. He showed us that the death undergone by means of contact with the Lamb of God is one to be sought, not feared: the death to self that acknowledges Christ as Lord and allows Him to be manifest in us by allowing our whole person to be taken over by Him for His purposes.

For the disciple aware of his own sinfulness, there is still that apprehension that overcomes anyone in the presence of the holy, much in the same way we saw it in the figures of Moses, Gideon, and Isaiah. We see it also in the figure of Saint Peter when he realizes the power of Jesus' presence at the miraculous catch of fish, and when Peter falls down on his knees and exclaims to the Lord, "Depart from me, Lord, for I am a sinful man!" (Lk 5:8). Still, it is clear that the negation of self that springs from being in the Lord's presence is not only because of sin; instead, it is the kind of self-negation that consists in wanting to be totally possessed by the Lord so as to be able to exclaim with Saint Paul: "I live, no longer I, but Christ lives in me" (Gal 2:20).

JESUS AS THE EXEMPLAR OF HOLINESS

The huge surprise for the human race with the appearance among us of God's own holiness in the person of Jesus Christ is the fact that this negation of self is not merely the reaction of the human person before the presence of God's holiness. Rather, this negation of self appears in Christ as the very pattern of God's own holiness itself. As Hans Urs von Balthasar points out, the "meaning of the Incarnation, of Jesus' manhood, is first borne in upon us as a not-doing, a not-ful-filling, a not-carrying-out of his own will." This is reflected in Jesus' words, "I have come down from heaven to do not my own will, but the will of him who sent me" (Jn 6:38).[5] Balthasar then accumulates an impressive collection of similar declarations of Jesus as found in the Gospel of John:

> The negation is primary. The Son can do nothing of himself (Jn 5:19, 30); he cannot speak on his own authority (7:17; 12:49; 14:10). And he does not do his own will (5:30; 6:38), although he has a will of his own (5:21; 17:24; 21:22) and so cannot be described as a vacuum in which God exists ... . It is of the essence of the Son to receive life (5:26), insight (3:11), spirit (3:34-35), word (3:34; 14:24), will (5:30), deed (6:9), doctrine (7:16), work (14:10), and glorification (8:54; 17:22, 24) from another, from the Father.[6]

It is evident that Jesus' essential posture of self-negation cannot be because of sin: certainly not because of any personal sin committed by Him, but not even because of His having taken upon Himself the sin of the world. This taking on the sin of the world does have something to do with the fact that His essential self-negation will take the form of His death on the Cross, but the self-negation itself is something even more profound. It is the appearance in human form of His eternal modality of being, even as the pre-existent Son. Unlike the eternal Father, the Son possesses the divine nature *as received from Another*. As Balthasar continues in his reflection, "If in him 'having' were for one moment to cease to be 'receiving,' to become a radically

---

[5] H. urs von Balthasar, *A Theology of History* (San Francisco: Ignatius Press, 1994), 29.

[6] Ibid., 29-30.

independent disposal of himself, he would in that moment cease to be the Father's Son, would have forfeited all claim to be believed, and would have to call on men not to believe him" (10:37).[7]

Like John the Baptist, the priest often comes into contact with people who expect him to be somehow more than human, and sometimes people address him as if he possessed holiness as an attribute of his own personality. The challenge in moments such as these is to respond in the same way as John did—or, for that matter in the same way that Jesus himself did—not merely as a show of humility but out of a recognition of the truth that such holiness, by its very nature, excludes the jealous possession of anything, but consists essentially in being radically dispossessed of self and oriented toward the Other who is the only ground of holiness. Holiness, as such, can never be claimed, and there is a certain way in which it cannot even be sought for itself, since it *is* precisely the absence of any such self-referential focus. As the priest is aware of standing before others in the person of Christ, he must also be aware that Christ Himself stands as the personification of radical negation of self: the One who receives his existence as something radically owed to Another, and who passes from that reception to the utter gift of self rather than holding on to what he has been given. The priest is called to allow that manner of existing to be the pattern of his prayer as well as of his whole way of life.

THE PRIEST AS "NOT I"

Since Jesus is the revelation of that "otherness" of God that is essential to the very definition of holiness, Jesus' own example of self-negation, so different from the attitudes of this world's children, stands at the core of any Christian spirituality. Saint John of the Cross conveys that same message even as he laments the extraordinary penances and pious exercises that some individuals undertake in trying to be holy, saying that "these practices are insufficient if a person does not diligently strive to deny his appetites. If these people would attempt to devote only half of that energy to the renunciation of their desires, they would profit more in a month than in years

---

[7] Ibid., 30.

with all these other exercises."[8] Likewise, Saint Ignatius of Loyola's "Principle and Foundation" begins by counseling the follower of his Spiritual Exercises to become "indifferent to all created things as far as they are subject to the liberty of our free will and not forbidden," not even desiring health over sickness, wealth over poverty, or longevity over a short life except insofar as it is conducive to our last end.[9] Parallels could no doubt be found in any classic of any school of Christian spirituality.

Even so, for the priest this same essentially Christian negation of self has a particular urgency and a particular form. Precisely because he has to stand before Christ's flock *in persona Christi*, he is always at risk of obscuring Christ's presence and becoming an obstacle whenever it is his own ego, rather than Christ's own identity, that he puts forward.

Nowhere is the need for a real divesture of self more evident than in the proper celebration of the Sacred Liturgy. In the Rite of Ordination itself, the prostration of the candidates speaks eloquently of the fact that the priest must first divest himself of his own ego in order to assume a new identity: an identity which—like Christ's own divine Personhood—can never be possessed without being received at the same time. While the new identity does become *his* identity, it is an essentially relational one, and similarly to the dynamic found within the Trinitarian life itself, it is the relationships that constitute the identity. This radical divesture of self and orientation toward the Other has the form of the Cross: on the vertical plane, it is lived between him and God, while on a horizontal level, his self-negation

---

[8] Saint John of the Cross, *Ascent of Mount Carmel,* Cited in T. Dubay, *Fire Within: St. Teresa of Avila, St. John of the Cross, and the Gospel—on Prayer* (San Franciso: Ignatius Press, 1989), 137. An excellent treatment of "The Freedom of Detachment" in these Carmelite writers' works extends from 131-157.

[9] Many different translations of the Spiritual Exercises are available, but Ignatius' autograph refers to this important paragraph as "Principio y Fundamento," and uses the phrase "indiferentes a todas las cosas criadas"; I have therefore kept the term "indifference" here, despite the fact that it requires explanation without which it might easily be misunderstood as a kind of apathy rather than as a healthy detachment. My base text was *Exercitia Spiritualia Sancti Ignatii de Loyola et eorum Directoria* (Matriti: Typis Successorum Rivadeneyrae, 1919), 250-251.

takes the form of his availability for the faithful. As Pope John Paul II wrote in the Apostolic Exhortation *Pastores dabo vobis*:

> Through the priesthood which arises from the depths of the ineffable mystery of God, that is, from the love of the Father, the grace of Jesus Christ and the Holy Spirit's gift of unity, the priest sacramentally enters into communion with the Bishop and with other priests in order to serve the People of God who are the Church.[10]

The essential matter and form of the sacrament of Order, the imposition of hands and the Prayer of Ordination, express concretely the reception of this new identity as bestowed upon the priest rather than elaborated by him, and also the consequent relationship of dependency that he has upon the bishop, apart from whom he cannot function. It is not as if his priesthood were merely an extension of the bishop's own; it is by Christ's power, not the bishop's, that he will confect the Eucharist and forgive sins. Even so, the priest receives these powers in such a way that they can only by exercised in a dependence on the bishop, together with whom all priests of the local Church form one Presbyterate, as a consequence not merely of their free association, but of their common sacramental bond.[11]

The relationship to the bishop that begins with this sacred action is essential to the personal holiness of the priest throughout his life. This is because it establishes the framework for obedience that the candidate pledged within the Ordination Rite just before the Litany and the Laying on of Hands. This ecclesial obedience is not merely an efficient way of marshalling all of the human resources of the Diocese to function in harmony. Nor is the value of priestly obedience absolutely dependent on the prudential content of the command that the bishop may give him in any given instance, nor even in the sum total of all such instances. Instead, the value of priestly obedience lies principally in the divestment of self that it expresses and brings about.

---

[10] Pope John Paul II, Apostolic Exhortation *Pastores Dabo Vobis*, March 25, 1992 (Rome: Libreria Editrice Vaticana), no. 12, accessed February 13, 2010, http://www.vatican.va/holy_father/john_paul_ii/apost_exhortations/documents/hf_jp-ii_exh_25031992_pastores-dabo-vobis_en.html.

[11] Cf. *Lumen Gentium*, no. 28; *Presbyterorum Ordinis*, no. 8.

Conversely, the act of trust that priestly obedience entails is not principally trust in the human judgment of the bishop. Rather, it is an act of trust that our genuine divestment of self-will makes us docile instruments in the hands of a God whom we see in the Scriptures as working His will for His people even through the commands of an unknowing and faithless pagan emperor—as Isaiah prophesied concerning Cyrus of Persia (Is 44:28-45:25). If God can do that, then all the more easily can He work His will in the life of the priest through the direction of a bishop even in the least favorable circumstances, namely when the bishop may be misinformed or mistaken about some factor affecting his assignment of the priest. Of course, this is not to say that priestly obedience should ever induce the priest to refrain from sharing with the bishop his own insights concerning the use of his talents, or that any obedience should ever lead to his violation of a higher law of God or of the Church's supreme authority.

Immediately after the Prayer of Ordination is a gesture that will be repeated by the priest himself every time he prepares to celebrate the Eucharist: namely, his putting on of the stole and chasuble. Pope Benedict XVI offered a beautiful reflection on the meaning of this daily gesture in his homily for the Chrism Mass in 2007:

> This event, the "putting on of Christ," is demonstrated again and again at every Holy Mass by the putting on of liturgical vestments. Vesting ourselves in them must be more than an external event: it means entering ever anew into the "yes" of our office—into that "no longer I" of Baptism which Ordination to the priesthood gives to us in a new way and at the same time asks of us.[12]

Also very telling in this same respect will be the way in which the priest does or does not observe the liturgical norms and adhere to the prescribed texts. This is not merely a question of legalism, but of the desire to give himself over to a reality that he could not have brought about and does not pretend to construct on his own. It is unfortunate if a priest thinks that in order to make the Liturgy "relevant,"

---

[12] Pope Benedict XVI, Homily for the Chrism Mass, Saint Peter's Basilica, 5 April 2007, accessed February 13, 2010, http://www.vatican. va/holy_father/benedict_xvi/homilies/2007/documents/hf_ben-xvi_ hom_20070405_messa-crismale_en.html.

he needs to change the texts in places where no such innovation is invited by them. Of course it is dull if the priest simply recites a text as if it were a grocery list. But it would be no less dull if instead of enacting faithfully the one unique and unrepeatable drama of the Paschal Mystery, he were to replace it with a cheapened version of his own making.

Our Latin Church has always had a genius for juridical ordering of things, even with regard to the Sacred Liturgy. But the reverse side of that coin is a frequent tendency to look at things *only* in legal terms, failing to see the deeper meaning of our conformity with the Church's norms. I remember a conversation that I had with another priest at the time that my mother died. She was not Catholic, but she told me previously when she had been pre-arranging her funeral— before there was any thought of an immediate need—that she would like me to preside at her funeral if that were possible. When she died rather unexpectedly while I was visiting my hometown, I went about trying to seek permission to celebrate a Catholic Funeral Rite for her, as the norms stipulate. One priest seemed perplexed that I was so concerned about what he considered a legalistic detail: how could there be any law against my praying for my own mother? Certainly no one would ever fault me for doing it, so why was it necessary even to ask?

For me, the permission was not about legalism or exoneration from disciplinary action. It was about the nature of the Rite that I wanted to offer for my mother: not a personal prayer of mine, of the kind that I was certainly already offering, but a Rite of the Church that was not my own possession. While I am fairly confident that I had the right insight in that moment (as so often we seem to be able to think most clearly about the things of God when faced with the death of a loved one), there have been other times when I experienced the temptation to possessiveness that we priests can fall into all too often without even realizing it.

For most of us, it may be easier to avoid possessiveness with the goods of this world; as I often say to people who know just a little bit about life in the Church and ask me if I have a vow of poverty: "I don't need one!" But it is a far more serious thing, more destructive to our true priestly identity, to be possessive about the things of God. Precisely *who* can speak in jealous terms about *my* Mass, *my* Church building, *my* parishioners, *my* institution or school that the bishop has entrusted to *me?* Certainly not the "new man" whom Saint Paul challenged with the affirmation that *even you yourself* "are not your own. For you have been purchased at a price" (1 Cor 6:19-20). Even though Saint Paul was speaking in that context about sexual impurity, the imagery still seems apt here, for treating the things of God as if they could be possessed like earthly goods entails another kind of impurity, no less to be avoided.

A MAN SET APART

The word *holy* was shown to be rooted in both Hebrew and Greek terms that signify "setting apart." Thus, the first and indispensable dimension of this in the life of the priest has to be a "setting apart" from his own ego in order to belong totally to Another. He also receives from the Other an identity that one could never otherwise assume. The Roman Liturgy of Penance allows this "setting apart" to be expressed through the priest's own mouth in the words, "*I* absolve you from your sins," which only Christ Himself can ultimately utter, and also in the Eucharistic words of institution, "This is *my* Body. This is *my* Blood."

This certainly does not mean that the priest himself does *not* intend to forgive the sinner in his own right as well; when he is a penitent himself going to Confession, after all, he knows that he experiences reconciliation in the fullest sense. He experiences this when he really is convinced that the priest speaking in the name and in the person of Christ is not doing so as an inanimate mouthpiece, but as a man taken up in Christ so as to take on Christ's own attitude of forgiveness. And similarly, when he speaks the words of Eucharistic institution, he is invited to make once again the offering of *his own body and blood* in and through the sacred Host that he holds.

The priest knows that whether he is faithful to his calling or not in his own moral life, Christ can and does ensure the validity of the sacraments for the sake of his Church. But he knows also that if he lives in a way that contradicts the mysteries he celebrates, he stands convicted of being an impostor. In fact, he will probably feel a healthy twinge of conscience at the contradictions presented even by the daily sins and imperfections that he failed to avoid. He will be aware of anyone who happens to witness these sins or imperfections, and who may want to call into question not only this particular priest's integrity, but the very gift of the priesthood itself.

Still, he is called to take up the daily adventure of living in tension between two identities: that of the flawed servant of God who he is, and that of the image of Christ, which he is called to put on daily. In this, it is the integrity of his struggle more than its end result that counts. There is a vast difference between one who stands up on his own power to pose as something that he is not, and one who stands up by God's power to allow himself to become more than he is. The first has its prototype in Satan's fall into everlasting death. The second finds its foundation in the Son's self-emptying before the Father who fills Him with His very being. This kind of divesture of self, so as to live the new identity that God bestows, might be considered the masculine counterpart of Mary's "yes." It is another way in which the Holy Spirit brings Christ to birth in human hearts.

In the living out of the priestly vocation, the divesture of self in order to take on the new priestly identity bestowed on him is not only a matter between the priest and God; it also concerns his relationship with the people entrusted to his care. I remember, when I was about to be ordained to the priesthood, a priest who already spent some years in priestly ministry said to me, "If you listen to the people, they will draw your priesthood out of you." In the years since then, I have found that to be true not only in parochial ministry, but also in seminary teaching and formation, and even in work as an official in the Roman Curia. I cannot say that I was always listening as I should, but whenever I did, it was the needs of God's people more than any abstract preparation that always showed me the meaning of being a priest in terms of flesh and blood.

Very often, one simple, visible sign that opens up the very possibility for such a dialogue between the people and us is our clerical clothing. As one who is "set apart," the priest distinguishes himself from the people in a visible way, not to stand above them, but to be in service to them. Paradoxically, then, this sign of his being "set apart" is also a sign that strengthens his unity with them. The priest, who because of his decision to wear clerical clothing, finds himself entering into friendly conversations with strangers, anointing a heart attack victim in a train station, or hearing a confession in an airport. He also finds that he, in a very different but mysterious way, suffered an insult that was really, even if unconsciously, uttered by some poor soul as intended for Christ Himself. The priest knows that while it is not wrong to spend recreation time without wearing clerical dress, neither is it ever a bad choice to wear it even outside of assigned priestly duties, as a sign of that distinctness of his priestly vocation that is not so much a "setting apart *from*" as it is a "setting apart *for*." The Second Vatican Council taught of this setting apart in an eloquent way in its *Decree on the Ministry and Life of Priests:*

> Priests of the New Testament, by their vocation and ordination, are in a certain sense set apart in the bosom of the People of God. However, they are not to be separated from the People of God or from any person; but they are to be totally dedicated to the work for which the Lord has chosen them. They cannot be ministers of Christ unless they be witnesses and dispensers of a life other than earthly life. But they cannot be of service to men if they remain strangers to the life and conditions of men.[13]

Each day the priest, who is attentive to the Lord's promptings, will know that the Lord extends to them the same invitation that we see Him giving to the disciples in the Gospel: "Come away by yourselves to a deserted place and rest a while" (Mk 6:31). The disciples knew from Jesus' own example that His going away "to a deserted place" (*eis erêmon topon*: cf. also Mk 1:35) was not merely a moment of leisure, but a "setting apart" of Himself once again to be present to the Father, who refreshes His soul and renews Him for the continuation of His mission. Interestingly, the Gospel of Mark shows Jesus inviting his disciples to such solitude precisely in a moment when the invitation will not be fulfilled because of the needy crowds coming even to that place in great numbers "like sheep without a shepherd" (Mk 6:34). Sometimes in priestly service, the scene will be repeated; a good intention to make time for prayer will be preempted by an unexpected pastoral need. Yet even when this happens, there seems no doubt that the desire to come to that "deserted place" to be alone with God has mysteriously been fulfilled after all. If that desire were not present, his pastoral care might have degenerated into self-interested activism. Instead, because of his desire to spend time apart

---

[13] *Presbyterorum Ordinis*, no. 3.

with God, he is still doing just that by feeding the flock that the Lord sends him.

LETTING THE LIGHT SHINE

If everything discussed up to now focused on the "setting apart" of the priest as the essence of priestly "holiness," and if that setting apart entails, first of all, a divesture of one's own ego, there is one important caution that seems necessary if this notion of self-negation is not to be misunderstood. The specific danger to be avoided here is that of "Quietism": namely, a kind of psychical self-annihilation akin to the spiritual attitude cultivated by some Eastern religions, by which one strives for the total inactivity of the mind and will, with the conviction that such inactivity itself consists in the blessedness being sought.[14] In the Eastern religions, the idea of *nirvana* entails a sort of escape from the perceived illusory character of visible things. Similarly, a misguided Christian Quietism so devalues human action that it leaves all the work to God and fails to take up the challenge of claiming this present world for Christ.

Certainly, and especially in twenty-first century America, it requires great trust in the Lord and solid formation in Biblical and ecclesial faith to be willing to let go of one's own ego in the manner that the priesthood of Jesus Christ demands of us. Nevertheless, it would be a terrible distortion if the pretense of holy trust were to become a cloak for apathy or cowardice. The Lord who takes posses-sion of us still continues to say, "I have come to set the earth on fire, and how I wish it were already blazing!" (Lk 12:49). The divesture of self that was mentioned earlier, then, does not call for the cessation of activity, but for the readiness to undertake any kind and any amount of activity needed in order to further the Kingdom of God.

On a superficial reading, there are some New Testament passages that might seem to contradict the expressed imperative of surrendering

---

[14] E. Pace, "Quietism," *The Catholic Encyclopedia*, vol. 12 (New York: Robert Appleton Company, 1911), accessed February 15, 2010, http://www.newadvent.org/cathen/12608c.htm.

one's ego, seen in some other passages already mentioned. In the Sermon on the Mount, we hear Jesus' words to the disciples:

> You are the light of the world. A city set on a mountain cannot be hidden. Nor do they light a lamp and then put it under a bushel basket; it is set on a lampstand, where it gives light to all in the house. Just so, your light must shine before others, that they may see your good deeds and glorify your heavenly Father (Mt 5:14-16).

Saint Paul, in turn, was not afraid to say to the Corinthians, "Become imitators of me as I am of Christ" (1 Cor 11:1).

How can these imperatives for Christ's messengers in this world be reconciled: "surrender yourself" on the one hand, and "put yourself forward," in effect, on the other? It seems that the best possible rubric into which these seemingly contradictory commands fit intelligibly is to be found in the dying and the rising of Christ: the priest is called to be the icon of Christ *both Crucified and Risen*. In the Crucified One, he sees the invitation to hand himself over without reservations, and to allow himself to be divested of his ego in order to belong to the One who calls him, and also to the flock entrusted to him. But in the Risen One, he sees that it is precisely to the One who thus laid Himself down that "[a]ll power in heaven and on earth has been given" (Mt 28:18), the power to handle serpents and all the forces of evil without being harmed (Mk 16:17-18), the power to preach repentance for the forgiveness of sins to all the nations (Lk 24:47), the power to achieve the ultimate conquest over the world (John 16:33). And, as the one who is commissioned to stand in the midst of God's people *in persona Christi*, the priest—even amid the humility that he is called to cultivate daily through the laying down of himself—is ultimately unfaithful to his mission if he fails to claim that power over this world—and especially over human hearts—that belongs to the Risen Christ.

Saint Paul wrote to the Corinthians about how they should live in persecution: "always carrying about in the body the dying of Jesus, so that the life of Jesus will also be made manifest in our body" (2 Cor 4:10). All the more so, then, in the life of the priest, does this divesture of self have as its goal the manifestation of the power of Christ Risen from the dead. In some of the saintly priests of our own time, we witnessed the extraordinary power wielded by men who live effectively within this tension between the two identities: their own ego they choose freely not to assert, and the "I" of the Lord Jesus that they allow to speak to others through their own person. The power of God's love shines through the very frailty of the men, as we saw with a particular vividness in those days when the ailing John Paul II stood at his window, and we were able to read the message of the Cross of Christ written in living flesh and blood in front of us.

The figure of John Paul II also marks a moment in history that I think exemplifies most clearly this paradoxical power of the man who lives the pattern of Jesus' own negation of himself before the Father. John Paul laid his humanity down at the disposal Christ, then stood up to the powers of this world, not asserting his own ego but pointing to the world's Savior. And when he did, those of us who are old enough to remember those days saw a spectacle that was no less amazing than the Biblical story of Jericho. John Paul sounded the trumpet that toppled the walls of the godless empire of Communism that held half of Europe in its grip for half a century, with his own Poland being the first domino to fall.

As long as history goes on, misguided human beings will intermittently rebuild the walls of Jericho, but God's trumpets are still being placed into the hands of the ones He calls: those willing to lay down their egos along with the weapons of this world, so as to be able to wield a power that is not their own, and not of this world. Our contemporaries have grown bored with those who peddle nothing more than their own ideas or their own personalities. But it will never grow bored of those priests who really do live their lives with Jesus and share with others what they heard from Jesus. These are the meek who will inherit the earth. And even though they are called to renounce the very tools that the world uses to force people into its own mold, they are the ones who will transform the world *from the inside out.* They are heirs of God's words to Jeremiah: "Then the LORD extended his hand and touched my mouth, saying, See, I place *my* words in *your* mouth! This day I set you over nations and over kingdoms, to root up and to tear down, to destroy and to demolish, to build and to plant" (Jer 1:9-10, italics added).

REFLECTION QUESTIONS

1. What concrete expressions or descriptions come into your mind as exemplary of the concept of "holiness"? Have you seen any examples that others may have identified with holiness, but which you do not believe truly manifest it? What are the prerequisites for living a life of holiness: what personal attributes need to be cultivated, and what is needed from outside of the self?

2. What reactions arise from an authentic encounter with holiness: Joy? Guilt? Gratitude? Supplication? Besides the reactions of Moses, Gideon, Peter, and others to God's holiness as narrated in the Bible, what other examples of trepidation before God's presence can you remember from Sacred Scripture? What examples have you witnessed in your own life?

3. How is it possible to distinguish between a negation of self that is an unhealthy sort of "martyrdom," and that which is a true imitation of Christ? Even at the same time that Christian faith calls for the emptying of self, how does it also enrich the self? Do you find the words "detachment" and "indifference," as used by the spiritual writers mentioned, appealing or repugnant? Would you perhaps use a different term for the same reality?

4. What is the relationship between clerical attire and vestments, on the one hand, and holiness, on the other? Which aspects of the liturgical celebration are not affected by the holiness of the priest, and which aspects are? What is the relationship between the holiness of priests and the holiness of the lay faithful?

SUGGESTED READINGS

Balthasar, Hans urs Von. "Christ's Mode of Time." In *A Theology of History*, 29-50. San Francisco: Ignatius, 1994.

_____. *Christian Meditation*. San Francisco: Ignatius, 1989.

_____. *Prayer*. San Francisco: Ignatius, 1986.

_____. "The Priestly State." In *The Christian State of Life*, 251-266. San Francisco: Ignatius, 1983.

Congregation for the Clergy. *Directory on the Ministry and Life of Priests*, 1994; esp. "The Identity of the Priest" (Chapter I, nn. 1-33) and "Priestly Spirituality" (Chapter II, nn. 34-68).

Dubay, Thomas. *Fire Within: St. Teresa of Avila, St. John of the Cross, and the Gospel—on Prayer.* San Franciso: Ignatius Press, 1989.

Hodgson, Robert, Jr. "Holiness (NT)." In *Anchor Bible Dictionary*, vol. 3, 249-254. New York: Doubleday, 1992.

John Paul II, Pope. Apostolic Exhortation *Pastores dabo vobis*, March 25, 1992. Chapter II, "He has Anointed Me and Sent Me Forth: The Nature and Mission of the Ministerial Priesthood," nn. 11-18; Chapter III, "The Spirit of the Lord is Upon Me: The Spiritual Life of the Priest," nn. 19-33.

Lachowski, J. "Holiness (in the Bible)." In *New Catholic Encyclopedia*, vol. 7, 51-52. Washington, D.C.: Catholic University, 1967.

Vaulx, Jules de. "Holy." In *Dictionary of Biblical Theology*, ed. Xavier Leon-Dufour, 236-239. Ijamsville, MD: The Word Among Us Press, 1988.

Chapter Two

MEN OF THE WORD:
PRIESTS AND SCRIPTURE

Rev. Patrick J. Brady, S.T.D.

Then they said to each other, "Were not our hearts burning
(within us) while he spoke to us on the way and opened
the scriptures to us?" (Lk 24:32).

"Were not our hearts burning?" Every priest, bishop and deacon
that I know desires to lead congregations to be on fire for the Lord,
to find their hearts burning with love. The importance of Scripture
in the lives of the faithful, the importance of preaching in the life of
the Church is strongly recognized today—at least on the surface. Yet,
I dare say most of us, clerics and laity, still find it shocking or discom-
forting when we hear the words of the Fathers of the Second Vatican
Council: "[P]riests, as co-workers with their bishops, have the
primary duty of proclamation of the Gospel of God to all."[1] Almost
fifty years afterwards, this statement still surprises and shocks. What
about the Eucharist? What about the sacraments? What about sanctification of the people?

Pope Gregory the Great describes priests as heralds of the good
news:

Anyone ordained a priest undertakes the task of preaching,
so that with a loud cry he may go on ahead of the terrible
judge who follows. If, then, a priest does not know how
to preach, what kind of cry can such a dumb herald utter?
It was to bring this home that the Holy Spirit descended

---

[1] Second Vatican Council, *Presbyterorum Ordinis*, Dec. 7, 1965, no. 4.

in the form of tongues on the first pastors, for he causes those whom he has filled, to speak out spontaneously.[2]

Gregory considers the idea of a priest unable to preach as an oxymoron. Preaching is inseparable from priesthood, yet do we truly recognize that? A common question that I ask men entering the Seminary is: "Why do you want to become a priest?" Typical replies are: "I want to serve the Church" or "I want to celebrate the sacraments" or "I want to help people." None to my knowledge ever responded to me the bold declaration: "I want to preach."[3]

Priesthood is commonly acknowledged to be a participation in the threefold ministry of Jesus: the ministry of priest, prophet, and king. That is, sanctification through sacramental celebration, witnessing to the Word, and pastoral leadership. All are essential components of priestly ministry and priestly identity. We often separate these components in order to understand them. However, these three aspects are part of the one priesthood of Jesus Christ. They cannot be truly separated. All too often, we, who participate in the one priesthood of Jesus Christ, can lose sight or neglect one facet, thinking that we are properly enriching another. Nonetheless, the actual consequence of neglecting one aspect most often leads directly to the diminishing of all three aspects. Without conversion of heart and proper understanding, what becomes of the Eucharist? On an experiential level it can be reduced to magic, self-centered piety, or empty ritual. Without the Eucharist, to what does proclamation of the Word lead to: Humanism? Auto-cephasism? Navel-Gazing? The roles of priest, prophet, and king are fundamentally interconnected in the one priesthood of Jesus Christ.

Regrettably, some took the Second Vatican Council's proper recognition of the primacy of the Word as proof for an anti-sacramental ecclesiology, interpreting it as the authentication for a de-sacralization of the priesthood.[4] In practice this means losing an understanding of the sacred. "Functionality" becomes the only

---

[2] Gregory the Great, *Pastoral Rule*, II, 4.

[3] I owe the awareness of this insight to Charles E. Miller, *Ordained to Preach: A Theology and Practice of Preaching* (Eugene, OR: Stock Publishers, 1992), 10.

[4] For a development of this split in the understanding of priesthood cf. Benedict XVI, "The Ministry and Life of Priests," October 24, 1995, in

element by which priesthood is valued. Within this framework, a priest is understood functionally as servant to the community but not as one who sanctifies. Rather than a vocation—a way of life called by and directed toward God—they reduce priesthood to an occupation, one among many in society. Reacting to this reduction of priesthood to functionality, others have rejected or ignored this primary role of priest as proclaimer—viewing it as a creeping Protestantization of the Church or as outright heresy. They anchor their understanding of priesthood in a sacramental-ontological concept seeing priesthood as granted by the Lord through the mediation of the Church. They emphasize the cultic role of the priest but often set in to a neglect of a ministry of service. He is one who celebrates Mass and the sacraments—the Scriptures often an afterthought. He is one who is completely separate from the people. The old adage, "Chalices, not calluses," epitomizes such thinking. The majority of priests do not fall into either extreme. They can be found somewhere in the middle of a sliding scale. But why? Why do we function as we do?

When Pope Benedict inaugurated the Year for Priests, he stated it was to encourage priests to strive for spiritual perfection. He said it was also for the Church as a whole to rediscover and reinforce its knowledge of the indispensible gift of grace which priests represent. The subtitle for this Year for Priests is "The Faithfulness of Christ; The Faithfulness of Priests." I believe that the Holy Father is reminding us of the ministry of Jesus which was always faithful to the will of the Father. In doing so, he challenges his priests to hold Jesus' faithfulness as the model for their own lives. In order to properly exercise our ministry, in order to properly set ourselves on the path to holiness which flows from proper exercise of priestly ministry, it is beneficial, it is essential to return to the foundations of our priesthood and to freshly rediscover our identity. As Paul VI stated in *Ecclesiam Suam*:

> Preaching is the primary apostolate. Our ministry, Venerable Brethren, is before all else the ministry of the Word. We are well aware of this, but it is good to remind ourselves of it at the present time so as to give the right orientation to our pastoral activities. We must return to

The Essential Pope Benedict XVI, ed. John F. Thorton and Susan B. Varenne (New York: Harper Collins, 2007), 305-307.

the study, not of human eloquence of empty rhetoric, but
of the genuine are of proclaiming the Word of God.[5]

This series of lectures seeks to explore the nature of priesthood.
Our focus today is "Priest as Man of the Word." What does it mean
to be a man of the Word? What is the Word we proclaim? How do
we proclaim it? How does the Word relate to the Eucharist? How
does proclamation lead to our own holiness? I offer three texts for
reflection: Mark, Acts, and First Corinthians.

JESUS AS PREACHER (MK 1:35-39)

Any understanding of priesthood must begin with Christ. The
Gospel of Mark offers a very brief, yet significant passage concerning
the ministry of Jesus near the beginning of the Gospel. Jesus, having
performed many miracles in Capernaum, went out early to pray in
a place of solitude. This moment of solitude occurs after what Mark
offers as a typical day in Jesus' Galilean ministry, a day which was
also the first day of His public ministry. During that day: He had
cast out a demon in the Synagogue, healed Peter's mother-in-law,
and cared for all the ill and possessed who came to the house where
He was staying. Early the next morning, Jesus sought a place of solitude in order to pray. Although it was early, many sought Him out.
Peter leads a group that intrudes on Jesus' solitude and upon finding
Him, practically scolds Jesus for disappearing because everyone was
looking for Him. Jesus responds to Peter by stating, "Let us go on
to the nearby villages that I may preach there also. For this purpose
have I come" (Mk 1:38).

Jesus states that His mission is to preach. Note that He does
not say He has come to preach exclusively. This does not mean that
Jesus came simply to talk, that He did not perform miracles, or offer
Himself on the Cross, or celebrate a Eucharistic banquet. Nor does
it mean that these things were not part of His ministry. Certainly
the acts of healing, which are a token and a beginning of the future
kingdom, also are part of His vocation. Later he announces that He
came to give His life as ransom to the many (Mk 10:45). His words
and deeds are bound together.

---

[5] Paul VI, *Ecclesiam Suam,* no. 90.

The context of this pericope offers insight into how the words and deeds relate. Mark does not tell us directly the reason why everyone seeks Jesus that morning. The verb that Mark employs, *zêteô,* meaning "search" or "seek," has a negative connotation in the Gospel. It is used to describe Jesus' opponents seeking Him out (Mk 11:18; 12:12; 14:1) and when people misunderstand Him (Mk 3:32; 8:11-12). The use of *zêteô* here implies that those seeking Jesus were seeking Him for the wrong reasons. They seek His miraculous powers and not His lordship. They search for the deeds He performs and not the kingdom He announces. They do not understand who He is; this is because they see only the deeds and fail to listen and understand His words. For the crowd, the signs and miracles take on such primary importance that the Word can no longer be heard.

Why does Mark place this significant scene near the beginning of Jesus' public ministry; that is, why does Mark feel it necessary to show that the true mission of Jesus is to proclaim the kingdom? The answer lies with the fact that actions without words fall into misunderstanding. Without the word, signs lose their meaning. Rather than reveal the kingdom, the signs turn irrelevant, are reduced to magic, or become things that merely astonish. The so-called motif of the "messianic secret" coined by William Wrede[6] does not reflect an attempt by the early Church to reconcile their belief in Jesus as Messiah with His failure to make it known during His ministry; rather, it reveals that understanding the identity of Jesus can be distorted if all one does is see the miracles.

Three times on His journey to Jerusalem Jesus reveals that His messiahship includes dying on a Cross. His mission can only be understood in light of the Cross. It is not accidental that the first time in Mark's narrative that a human recognizes Jesus' true identity as "Son of God," it was at the time of His death (Mk 15:39). His preaching directs us to the Cross and helps us understand it. Jesus' death, properly understood, is the summit of His preaching. In a similar way, the Eucharistic liturgy is the summit of priestly preaching.

> The preaching of Jesus should be called "sacramental"
> [...] his word bears in itself the reality of the incarnation

---

[6] Cf. William Wrede, *Das Messiasgeheimnis in den Evanglien,* 1901 (English translation: *The Messianic Secret,* 1971).

and theme of the cross and resurrection. And in this deep way word and action are combined. It indicates the reciprocity of preaching and the Eucharist for the Church, but also of preaching and witness that is lived and suffered.[7]

Words and signs are inseparable. Whenever the signs are interpreted as mere wonders, without grasping their content as revelation, their value is then diminished or distorted. Thus Jesus rejects the challenge of the Pharisees seeking (*zêteô*) a sign (Mk 8:11). Miracles do not automatically produce faith. In Mark's Gospel, miracles are a manifestation of God's power, but they are experienced by people of faith, like the paralytic, the woman hemorrhaging, and the man born blind (Mk 2:5; 5:34; 10:52).

What does Jesus proclaim? Mark offers us a summarization of His preaching: "Jesus came to Galilee proclaiming the gospel of God: 'This is the time of fulfillment. The kingdom of God is at hand. Repent, and believe in the gospel'" (Mk 1:14-15). What does it mean to announce the kingdom? It means to call others to make the living, powerful, and present God the priority of their lives. Jesus does not consider preaching to be merely an intellectual activity. His word demands action. They create reality. They call for a conversion of heart, a different way of seeing and living in the world, a way that is built on trust and dependency on God. The proper response to the proclamation of the Word disposes people to truly hear the message in the miracles. Without the proper response to announcement of the kingdom, people "look and see but not perceive, and hear and listen but not understand" (Mk 4:12).

Jesus does not communicate content independent of His person. Mark's opening phrase, "The Gospel of Jesus Christ" (Mk 1:1) should not be understood as merely an objective genitive, the good news about Jesus; nor should it be understood as merely a subjective genitive, the good news which Jesus told us; rather, it is a genitive of apposition—Jesus embodies the good news. He is more than a rabbi. He is the kingdom in person. The decision demanded by Him is a decision to encounter Him, to be in relationship with Him, to

---

[7] Benedict XVI, *Life and Ministry of Priests*, 309.

believe in Him. Preaching does not just deal with words, but the Word. Jesus is the *logos*, the eternal Word of the Father.

> In times past, God spoke in partial and various ways to our ancestors through the prophets; in these last days, he spoke to us through a son, whom he made heir of all things and through whom he created the universe, who is the refulgence of his glory, the very imprint of his being, and who sustains all things by his mighty word (Heb 1:1-3).

The Gospel of Mark—and the rest of Scripture—leads us to encounter the person of Christ, not just a collection of ideas.

Returning to the encounter between Jesus and Peter, we should note that Jesus sought time for prayer before He went to the other towns and villages. Mark tells us that Jesus sought out a deserted place, the *erêmon topon* (Mk 1:35). The use of *erêmos* recalls the motif of the wilderness as a privileged place for encountering God. Mark also places the verb *to pray* in the imperfect tense. This tense connotes an ongoing or repeated action. Early morning daily prayer was the common practice of Jewish piety.[8] Since this pericope occurs at the end of what Mark seems to be portraying as a typical day in the life of Jesus, we can assume that Mark intends us to see this prayer as typical in Jesus' ministry. In this brief mention of Jesus at prayer, no words are mentioned. (Neither does Mark record any words in his second account of Jesus at prayer: when, after the feeding of the five thousand, he went up the mountain—another place of privileged encounter with God (Mk 6:46). For Mark, prayer should be understood primarily as being in the presence of God.[9] That is, before Jesus goes out to preach, He spends time in prayer with the Father. Preaching presumes prayer.

One last item from this pericope is that preaching is joined with the expelling of demons. Jesus' proclamation does not take place in a beautiful and healthy world but one dominated by demons.[10] For His first miracle in Mark's narrative, Jesus enters the Capernaum synagogue and expels a demon possessing a man. This miracle occurs

---

[8] Cf. John R. Donahue and Daniel Harrington, *The Gospel of Mark*, Sacra Pagina (Collegeville: Michael Glazier, 2002), 87.

[9] Cf. Donahue and Harrington, *The Gospel of Mark*, 212.

[10] Benedict XVI, *The Ministry and Life of Priests*, 308.

immediately following Mark's summary of Jesus' proclamation that the kingdom is at hand. The proclamation of the Gospel implants freedom in the world. The announcement of the kingdom liberates humanity from the dominion of evil and restores the relationship with God.

THE EARLY CHURCH PREACHES CHRIST
(ACTS 8:26-39)

After the resurrection, the Apostles made the proclamation of the Word a priority in their mission. When issues arose within the early Church over the fair distribution of aid to the widows, Luke informs us that the Twelve called the community of believers together and said:

> It is not right for us to neglect the word of God to serve at table. Brothers, select from among you seven reputable men, filled with the Spirit and wisdom, whom we shall appoint to this task, whereas we shall devote ourselves to prayer and to the ministry of the word (Acts 6:1-4).

For the Apostles, other important works should not interfere with their primary duty of proclaiming the Word. Interestingly, Luke only informs us about the ministry of only two of the seven deacons: Stephen and Phillip. Neither one is portrayed as caring for the widows but proclaiming the good news. Acts 8 offers a wonderful account in the slenderest of vignettes showing Phillip, driven by the Spirit, unfolding the Scriptures and proclaiming Jesus.

> Philip ran up and heard him [The Ethiopian Eunuch] reading Isaiah the prophet and said, "Do you understand what you are reading?" He replied, "How can I, unless someone instructs me?" [...] Then Philip opened his mouth and, beginning with this scripture passage, he proclaimed Jesus to him (Acts 8:30-31, 35).

This scene shows us the connection between the Scriptures and Christ. The Scriptures are not merely ancient words preserved in ancient texts, but Christ present to us. Whenever we read a text, what we are reading does not come from a nebulous "anywhere," but from a specific author, a specific person. If we truly seek to understand and respond to a communication, then we are not simply responding to a fact communicated, but to the person communicating. Communication is an irreducibly interpersonal event. If we truly hold that the Scriptures are God's self-communication, we are responding not merely to a dogma or an idea, but to God Himself.

This is the reason the Church uses the polyvalent expression "proclaim the Word." First and foremost "Word" refers to the eternal *logos*, the second person of the Trinity. Secondly, it refers to Scriptures, in which we truly encounter the divine *logos*. In order for us to proclaim Christ we need to be immersed in the Scriptures. Jerome's much quoted aphorism "ignorance of the Scriptures is ignorance of Christ" challenges all Christians to immerse themselves in the Scriptures, particularly those ordained to proclaim the Word.

Luke uses a septuagintal phrase "opened his mouth" (*avoixas* [...] *to stoma autou*, Acts 8:35) to describe Phillip's proclaiming Christ. This phrase was used in the Septuagint for solemn (Jb 11:36; 33:2; 35:6) or prophetic discourse (Ex 4:12, 15; Ez 3:27; 29:21; 33:22). When Phillip unfolds the Scriptures he is not speaking his own words nor offering his own interpretation. He is led by the Spirit to proclaim the Words of God.

Luke's description of Phillip's preaching, "beginning with this scripture passage, he proclaimed Jesus to him," purposely parallels the scene of Jesus on the road to Emmaus: "Then beginning with Moses and all the prophets, he interpreted to them what referred to him in all the scriptures" (Lk 24:27). The preaching of the early Church is a continuation of the preaching of Jesus.

The narrative of Phillip and the Eunuch culminates with the Baptism of the Eunuch. The scene at Emmaus with Jesus unfolding the Scriptures culminates in the breaking of the bread. Proclaiming the Word and reception of the sacraments are inherently linked. Pope Benedict at the Synod of Bishops on Scripture states:

> We all sense how necessary it is to place the Word of God at the center of our life, to welcome Christ as our only Redeemer, as the kingdom of God in person, to allow his light to enliven every sphere of humanity: from the family to the school, to work, to free time and to other sectors of society and of our life. Participating in the celebration

of the Eucharist, we are always aware of the close bond
which exists between the announcement of the Word of
God and the Eucharistic Sacrifice: It is the same mystery
which is offered for our contemplation.[11]

Proclaiming the Word leads to the sacraments. It allows people
to be open to and properly disposed toward the sacraments. So they
can truly ask with the Eunuch, "What is to prevent my being baptized?" (Act 8:36). The Word of God receives His full embodiment
in creation; above all, in the sacrament of the Eucharist. It is there
that the Word becomes flesh and allows us not simply to see Him,
but to touch Him with our own hands and make Him part of our
own body. If we proclaim the kingdom, the Eucharist offers us the
true foretaste of the kingdom. Properly understood, the Eucharist is
the proclamation par excellence of the kingdom. To separate it from
preaching is to empty preaching of its meaning.

Proclamation of the Word is not simply reading the Scriptural
texts aloud. The Eunuch read the texts but still required someone to
teach; to unfold the mysterious that can only be properly understood
by a believer. Preaching unfolds and makes present the words in a
concrete historical reality. The Scriptures require explanation and
study. Chrysostom said this: "Though the preacher may have great
ability (and this one would only find in a few), not even in this case
is he released from perpetual toil. For since preaching does not come
by nature, but by study."[12]

PAUL: SENT TO PREACH (1 COR 1:10-17)

Among those named Apostles, Paul is the most renowned for his
efforts of evangelization. In First Corinthians he states:

I give thanks (to God) that I baptized none of you [...]
For Christ did not send me to baptize but to preach the
gospel, and not with the wisdom of human eloquence,
so that the cross of Christ might not be emptied of its
meaning (1 Cor 1:14, 17).

---

[11] Benedict XVI, *Homily for Synod of Bishops on Scripture.*

[12] John Chrysostom, *On Priesthood*, V.5.

This is one of the most misused and abused Scriptural passages in the area of preaching. Some have taken this as an argument pitting preaching against sacraments. Others have taken it to deny the need for preparation in preaching. These shallow interpretations fail to explore the context of the passage. As the Scripture scholar Ben Witherington quips, "A text without context is just a pretext for what we want it to mean."[13] The problem in Corinthians stems from divisions caused by focusing on the person of the minister rather than the person of Christ; or more particularly, seeing the human person rather than the Spirit acting through them.

The first part of Paul's statement thanking God that he has not baptized refers to the gross misunderstanding of the meaning and significance of the sacraments, particularly Baptism. They are focused on the prestige of the minister rather than the power of the sacrament. Paul satirically offers thanks to God that he did few Baptisms. Not because he does not value Baptism or other sacraments but because his name cannot be used as a source of dividing the community through the sacramental life. The Corinthians seemed to be dividing themselves under the umbrellas of the sacramental ministers rather than experiencing the unity the grace of the sacrament should provoke.

We can see similar things today in our parishes. There is a natural human tendency to find prestige or authentication if a sacrament is received from the proper minister. To have received a sacrament from an important figure often becomes a source of boasting. Who would not boast, "I was confirmed by the Holy Father!" Apart from the issue of their use and abuse, why do some switch lines when a priest distributes communion in one, while a lay extraordinary minister distributes communion in another? Is the Eucharist somehow more real when received from the hands of the priest? What about the preference of bishop over priest, pope over bishop, in the reception of Baptism or Confirmation or Marriage? Such things can become a source of pride, a source of boasting that loses sight of the importance of the sacrament received. Even among priests this boasting can occur. When I was in Rome, some saw great prestige not in being ordained

---

[13] B. Witherington, *The Indelible Image: The Theological and Ethical Thought World of the New Testament*, vol. 1, *The Individual Witnesses* (Downers Grove: Intervarsity Press 2009), 41.

to the diaconate, but because they were ordained by the pope or a member of the Roman Curia. What is being celebrated when people boast of these things—the sacrament that conforms one to the person of Jesus and into the mysteries of the kingdom, or the prestige that places oneself above others? Focus on the minister rather than the sacrament leads to division within the one family of God. The boast that "my child was baptized by the bishop" can also imply that since yours was not, he or she is somehow less. This seems to be the heart of Paul's critique—"there are rivalries among you. I mean that each of you is saying, 'I belong to Paul,' or 'I belong to Apollos,' or 'I belong to Kephas,' or 'I belong to Christ'" (1 Cor 1:11-12). These same problems occurred in the time of John Chrysostom.

> For to begin with, the majority of those who are under the preachers' charge [...] disdaining the part of learners, they assume instead the attitude of those who sit and look on at the public games; [...] some attach themselves to one, and some to another, so here also men are divided, and become the partisans now of this teacher, now of that, listening to them with a view to favor or spite.[14]

For Paul the solution to the divisions—to the "I" statements—is authentic preaching, a focus on his primary apostolic charge. Only when Christ is proclaimed can Paul's charge be realized: "that all of you agree in what you say, and that there be no divisions among you, but that you be united in the same mind and in the same purpose"(1 Cor 1:10). Authentic preaching gives context to the sacraments. As Paul recognizes, "everyone who calls on the name of the Lord will be saved. But how can they call on him in whom they have not believed? And how can they believe in him of whom they have not heard? And how can they hear without someone to preach?" (Rom 10:13-14). Authentic preaching allows hearts and minds to be turned toward Christ and the Father so that believers recognize the grace God bestows on us in Jesus Christ (1 Cor 1:4). Authentic preaching creates community. It allows believers to recognize the sanctification they received in the sacraments; their call to be holy unites them "with all those everywhere who call upon the name of our Lord Jesus Christ" (1 Cor 1:2).

---

[14] John Chrysostom, *On Priesthood*, V.1.

But what is authentic preaching? How is it achieved? What are its characteristics? This is the topic Paul turns to in the second half of verse 17. For Paul, authentic preaching is not filled with the wisdom of human eloquence, an eloquence which results in the Cross of Christ being emptied of its meaning. Authentic preaching builds others' faith "not on human wisdom but on the power of God" (1 Cor 2:5). There are two observations we must make to properly understand his critique of inauthentic preaching.

The first observation is that Paul does not contrast reason and irrationality as different ways of brining listeners to the truth. We are not asked to have a frontal lobotomy or to check our brains at the door when we read the Scriptures in light of our faith. Nowhere does Paul call for an abandonment of human reason—the *sacrificium intellectus*. Indeed, Paul challenges us to the opposite. Paul does not call for a sacrifice of the intellect but its sanctification. "Do not conform yourselves to this age but be transformed by the renewal of your mind, that you may discern what is the will of God, what is good and pleasing and perfect" (Rom 12:2). To fully grasp Scripture, one needs to use the full capacity of one's intellect. However, one's ability to understand directly corresponds to acknowledging God. If we fail to accord glory to God, fail to recognize His works and wonders, focusing instead on human achievements, we become vain in our reasoning. What we think is wisdom is actually foolishness because we have replaced God with ourselves (Rom 2:20-23).

True wisdom, true understanding can only come from listening to the Word of God. As Pope Benedict said in his address to the Synod on Scripture:

> The Word of God is the foundation for everything, it is the true reality. And to be realistic, we must rely on this reality. We must change our notion that matter, solid things, things we can touch, are the most solid, most certain reality. We must change our concept of realism. The realist is he who recognizes the Word of God, in this apparently weak reality, as the foundation of all things. The realist is he who builds his life on the foundation

which is permanent (Sermon on Mount, permanent foundation).[15]

Authentic preaching, therefore, is rooted in the Scriptures; not in the latest movie, or a nice poem, or a presidential address. These things cannot substitute for the Scriptures. To do so reduces preaching to human wisdom and human foolishness. It is to the Scriptures that we must constantly return. Thus Paul charges Timothy:

> You have followed my teaching, way of life, purpose, faith, patience, love, endurance, persecutions, and sufferings [...] remain faithful to what you have learned and believed, because you know from whom you learned it, and that from infancy you have known (the) sacred scriptures, which are capable of giving you wisdom for salvation through faith in Christ Jesus. All scripture is inspired by God and is useful for teaching, for refutation, for correction, and for training in righteousness, so that one who belongs to God may be competent, equipped for every good work (2 Tm 3:10, 14-17).

The second observation is that Paul does not critique the use of rhetoric itself in proclaiming the Gospel. He does not espouse last-minute, nonsensical, stream-of-consciousness homilies that are noted more for their unstructured and aimless meandering than for conveying Christ. The work of preaching requires conscious work on the part of the priest. It is precisely that conscious laboring that leads to salvation. Paul exhorts Timothy:

> Until I arrive, attend to the reading, exhortation, and teaching. Do not neglect the gift you have, which was conferred on you through the prophetic word with the imposition of hands of the presbyterate [...] Attend to yourself and to your teaching; persevere in both tasks, for by doing so you will save both yourself and those who listen to you (1 Tm 4:13-14, 16).

It has been long recognized by scholars that Paul, in his own writings, employs all types of rhetorical techniques. In this very passage under consideration he employs rhetorical techniques. Note

---

[15] Cf. Pope Benedict, *Reflection at the First General Congregation*, Monday October 6, 2008.

the anaphoric gradation of the cries of allegiance that reaches a rhetorical climax in "Christ." Note the contrast between the "I" and the community of "same mind and opinion." Note the use of a series of rhetorical questions to put the Corinthians on their heels. The letter is replete with rhetorical devices and aids. Classic rhetorical arguments were built on three foundations: *ethos*, which is the character and authority of the person; *pathos*, which is the emotional engagement of the audience, and *logos*, which is the intellectual engagement of the audience. Throughout his letters, Paul effectively employs all three. He continuously refers to his own office and his own conduct, which the various churches witnessed in him. He is very aware of meeting the needs of his audience, praising and blaming when necessary, appealing to their bonds in Christ. Arguably he even changes his writing to Asiatic Greek when sending letters to the Colossians and Ephesians in Asia Minor.[16] His arguments appeal to the *logos* by delineating contrasting positions and showing the value of his and the weakness of his opponents—"they empty the cross."

The heart of Paul's critique in First Corinthians concerns the emphasis given to great speakers rather than the truth spoken. The Thessalonians are falling into divisions because they seem to root their faith in the rhetorical artistry of the human speaker, rather than in Jesus. They appreciate form over content. What he describes is the preacher's method in propagation of the Gospel. What Paul is denouncing is the valuing of artistry over truth, of seduction over reality. The problems of this type of rhetoric were recognized and widespread in the ancient world. Plato used strong words to criticize rhetoricians: "in the courts [...] nobody cares for truth [...] but [only] for that which is convincing [...] paying no attention to the truth."[17] Paul attacks any use of rhetoric which is more enamored with its own devices and brilliance than with the Cross, with Christ, and with authentic Christianity.

What is at stake is true conversion of heart. True faith comes from the power of the Spirit, not human trickery. Faith rests "not

---

[16] For the argument surrounding his use of style and the authenticity of Pauline authorship, cf. Ben Witherington, *The Letters to Philemon, the Colossians and the Ephesians: A Socio-Rhetorical Commentary on the Captivity Epistles* (Grand Rapids: Eerdmans, 2007), 1-37.

[17] Plato, *Phaedrus*, 272.

on human wisdom but on the power of God" (1 Cor 2:5). Attempts
by a preacher to supplant God's wisdom with his own artistry is to
supplant the work of the Spirit. This is a perennial danger for popular
speakers, particularly when they are viewed as more authoritative
than the Scriptures. In the worse case they empty the Gospel of the
Cross, as does Joel Olsteen and the prosperity gospel movement.
Thus the preacher should not preach "with words taught by human
wisdom, but with words taught by the Spirit, describing spiritual
realities in spiritual terms" (1 Cor 2:13).

One of the great maxims for preachers is not to preach oneself.
The Second Vatican Council document, *Presbyterorum Ordinis,* states
that, "The priest should never teach his own wisdom, but the Word
of God which urges truth and holiness."[18] The pulpit is not a place
to show off, nor is it to draw attention to the preacher. On a human
level this is an important caution. As Paul states: "For we do not
preach ourselves but Jesus Christ as Lord" (2 Cor 4:5). Theologically,
however, this maxim needs nuance. The effective preacher embodies
the Word of God. Paul states "we have renounced shameful, hidden
things; not acting deceitfully or falsifying the word of God, but by
the open declaration of the truth we commend ourselves to everyone's conscience in the sight of God" (2 Cor 4:2). The Word is part
of his being by ordination and should be by, prayer, study, and reflection. A priest proclaims Christ from the very depths of his priestly
identity.[19] Thus it is "no longer I who live but Christ lives in me"
(Gal 2:20). To cite Pope Benedict XVI:

> The ministry of the word demands the priest participation
> in the kenosis of Christ, his living and dying. The fact
> that the priest does not speak of himself, but bears the
> message of another, does not mean personal indifference,
> but rather the opposite—to lose oneself in Christ entails
> truly finding oneself and in being in communion with
> the Word of God in person. The paschal structure of "no
> longer "I" and yet of my true "I" shows how in the end
> the ministry of the Word, above and beyond all of the

---

[18] Second Vatican Council, *Prebyterorum ordinis,* no. 4.

[19] Cf Miller, *Ordained to Preach,* 12-13.

functional, penetrates into one's being and supposes the priesthood as sacrament.[20]

Congregations can tell when a priest reads a manufactured homily, or regurgitates another's ideas without having made them his own through prayer and reflection—the difference between preaching oneself and preaching Christ. Preaching is not reducible to a collection of ideas or to eloquent sound bites. Preaching must offer an encounter with the person of Christ. "Be imitators of me, as I am of Christ" (1 Cor 11:1).

Authentic preaching is rooted in the concept of "servant." Servant is a relational concept. This means the very essence of priesthood is relational. Being ordered to the service of the Lord constitutes the essence of priestly ministry. It defines priestly existence. Priests are the servants of Christ in order to be the servants of men. Thus Paul, slave of Jesus Christ, can say:

> I have made myself a slave to all so as to win over as many as possible. To the Jews I became like a Jew to win over Jews; to those under the law I became like one under the law—though I myself am not under the law—to win over those under the law. To those outside the law I became like one outside the law—though I am not outside God's law but within the law of Christ—to win over those outside the law. To the weak I became weak, to win over the weak. I have become all things to all, to save at least some. All this I do for the sake of the gospel, so that I too may have a share in it (1 Cor 9:19-23).

Priestly configuration to Christ is not opposed to service to the community but is the basis which alone gives it depth. An ontological conception of the priesthood cannot be set in opposition to functional activity; but rather, it creates a radicalness in serving which would be unthinkable in a purely profane activity.[21] Because priests belong to Christ, they belong in a radical way to humanity.

Authentic preaching is not something a preacher can boast about, since it is done in service. The Apostles and those who continue their work in the church today—bishops, priests and deacons—are

---

[20] Benedict XVI, *The Ministry and Life of Priests*, 310.

[21] Ibid., 317-318.

charged with the mission of authentic preaching. Thus Paul states: "If I preach the gospel, this is no reason for me to boast, for an obligation has been imposed on me, and woe to me if I do not preach it!" (1 Cor 9:16).

CONCLUSION

The fundamental question for this talk is, "What does it mean to be a man of the Word?" Reflecting upon Jesus, Phillip, and Paul, some consistent themes emerge: identity, prayer and work, and conformation to Christ. The Scriptures and Church documents consistently hold that the primary work of the priest is to proclaim. The determining priority of a priesthood that participates in the one priesthood of Christ is the proclamation of the Gospel. This is a matter of priestly identity and parish identity. In order to be faithful to our identity, we must constantly ask ourselves if this priority is truly reflected in the priorities that we make in our lives. For instance, if the homily offers a particularly priestly way of proclaiming the Word because of its intimate connection to the Eucharist, do we reflect that by the time we spend in preparation? Or is it simply another item among many in our calendar book, an item easily bounced for other things? Does our spiritual life focus on the many devotionals—which in themselves are good and every priest needs to suit his individual needs—to the neglect of the Scriptures and in particular the Liturgy of the Hours?

> Nourishing oneself with the Word of God is for her [the Church] the first and fundamental responsibility. In effect, of the proclamation of the Gospel constitutes her reason for being and her mission, it is indispensible that the Church know and live that which she proclaims, so that her preaching is credible, despite the weaknesses and poverty of her members (Pope Benedict, Synod on Scripture).

Do the organizations of the parish see proclamation as part of their mission? Take the typical parish youth organization: is it a vehicle for fostering the Gospel or a shadowy organization existing on the margins of the pastor's awareness? How about our schools: do they nourish students on the Word of God or simply offer a good secular education?

This fundamental responsibility of proclaiming the Word presumes prayer and study. Merely reading the Scriptures does not necessitate that we truly understood the Word of God. The danger is that we see only human words and do not find the true Actor within: the Holy Spirit. The danger is to fall into eisegesis, imposing ourselves into the Scriptures.

> [...] a good biblical exegesis requires both the historical critical method as well as the theological one, because the Holy Scripture is the Word of God in human words. This means that every text must be read and interpreted bearing in mind the unity of all of Scripture, the living tradition of the Church and the light of faith. If it is true that the Bible is also a literary work, rather, the great code of universal culture, it is also true that it must not be devoid of the divine element, but must always be read in the same Spirit in which it was written. Scientific exegesis and *lectio divina* therefore are both necessary and complementary for finding, through the literary and spiritual meaning, what God wishes to communicate to us today.[22]

There are those who can give all the right answers but do not see reality because they do not know the Savior. Origen, in a letter to his pupil, Gregory, (who would later become the bishop of Caeserea and called Thaumaturgus) stated:

> Study first of all the divine Scriptures. Study them I say. For we require to study the divine writings deeply, lest we should speak of them faster than we think; and while you study these divine works with a believing and God-pleasing intention, knock at that which is closed in them, and it shall be opened to you [...] And do not be content with knocking and seeking, for what is most necessary for understanding divine things is prayer.[23]

Learning without grace does not reach the heart. To be effective preachers the Word must truly exist in the priest's heart. The Liturgy

---

[22] Benedict XVI, *Angelus* Talk at Close of Synod of Bishops on Scripture.

[23] Origen, *Letter to Gregory*.

of the Hours is particularly appropriate for preachers revolving around the Psalms and reflections of the Fathers. It is an integral part of homiletic spirituality, uniting priests with the prayer of the Church whom they are called to serve.[24] It is "the prayer of the church, par excellence [...] destined to give rhythm to the days and times of the Christian year."[25]

It is only through contemplative prayer, attending to the depth of the Word, that we can truly convey it to others. At the Synod of Bishops held at the Vatican in October, 2008, one of the recommendations made over and over again by the bishops was the practice of *lectio divina*. As Athanasius charged, "You will not see anyone who is really striving after his advancement who is not given to spiritual reading. And as to him who neglects it, the fact will soon be observed by his progress" (Athanasius, *Easter Homily*). *Lectio divina* should be complemented by *lectio continua*, a continuous reading through the Scriptures, so that passages can be seen and prayed in their fuller context.

The primary duty of the priest is not an easy one. There are many dangers. The danger of imposing our words into the text can only be prevented by study undertaken in a spirit of humility which places the words in their historical, literary, canonical, and ecclesial context. We have that same danger of stopping at the human words, words from the past, words trapped in ancient history; and thus, fail to discover the Spirit speaking to us in living words. We have the danger of reacting to reception rather than faithfulness to the Scriptures. The great Apostle charges us:

> Always be ready to give an explanation to anyone who asks you for a reason for your hope, but do it with gentleness and reverence, keeping your conscience clear, so that, when you are maligned, those who defame your good conduct in Christ may themselves be put to shame. For it is better to suffer for doing good, if that be the will of God, than for doing evil (1 Pet 3:15-17).

---

[24] Miller, *Ordained to Preach*, 25.

[25] XII Ordinary General Assembly of the Synod of Bishops, Message to the People of God, October 24, 2008, 9.

Prayer and study have as their one focus "putting on Christ." Preaching calls for a deep conversion to the Word of God, a willingness to ponder the Word long and lovingly, giving flesh not only to the words, but through a way of life. Authentic preaching must come from the heart of the preacher. As Gregory the Great noted in his *Pastoral Rule:* "Every preacher should give forth a sound more by his deeds than by his words, and rather by good living imprint footsteps for men to follow than by speaking show them the way to walk in."[26]

Therefore authentic preaching requires the preacher to conform the entirety of his life to Christ. Preaching, of course, is not limited to the homily. It includes the evangelization that precedes and follows worship, as well as the teaching that accompanies it.[27] At the closing *Angelus* for the Synod of Bishops on Scripture, Benedict stated,

> To priests in particular the new media offer ever new and far-reaching pastoral possibilities, encouraging them to embody the universality of the Church's mission, to build a vast and real fellowship, and to testify in today's world to the new life which comes from hearing the Gospel of Jesus, the eternal Son who came among us for our salvation. At the same time, priests must always bear in mind that the ultimate fruitfulness of their ministry comes from Christ himself, encountered and listened to in prayer; proclaimed in preaching and lived witness; and known, loved and celebrated in the sacraments, especially the Holy Eucharist and Reconciliation.[28]

Just as Christ's life is the Gospel, so must the priest's life be. The faithfulness of Jesus reveals the Father's love to us. The faithful priest not only explains the Scriptures but unfolds them as a living and practiced reality. The life of a priest conformed to Christ is proclamation. Thus Peter charges:

> Whoever preaches, let it be with the words of God; whoever serves, let it be with the strength that God supplies, so that

---

[26] Gregory the Great, *Pastoral Rule*, II, 40.

[27] Cf. Second Vatican Council, *Sacrosanctum Concilium*, no. 9.

[28] Benedict XVI, "New Technologies, New Relationships. Promoting a Culture of Respect, Dialogue and Friendship," Message for the 43rd World Communications Day.

in all things God may be glorified through Jesus Christ, to whom belong glory and dominion forever and ever. Amen (1 Pt 4:11).

REFLECTION QUESTIONS

1. What is authentic preaching? How can "preach oneself" be properly understood and misunderstood? How does the daily life of the parish priest affect his preaching? How does the presence of the priest to his parishioners affect his preaching? What can priests do to ensure that their preaching is authentic?

2. How is the primary role of the priest—proclamation of the Word—reflected in their daily lives and in their parishes? What practices of a priest hinder their primary role? What practices and habits help foster proclaiming the Word? How do the various organizations of the parish reflect the priorities of the parish priest? Are there specific things that the parish as a whole can contribute to the priest's primary mission?

3. How does preaching relate to the sacraments, particularly the Eucharist? Should sacrament-based preaching include instruction, or only contain instructions? How does the Eucharistic setting make the homily different from other forms of preaching? How should this difference affect the structure of a homily? In what ways can the priest's own use of the sacrament of Reconciliation contribute to his proclaiming the Word?

4. How is proper integration of faith and reason essential for authentic preaching? What does prayer have to do with proclaiming the Word? What are the strengths and limitations of the academic study of the Scriptures? What does Spirit-guided preaching require on the part of the priest? What relationship should the priest have with the Church and *Magisterium* regarding his preaching?

SUGGESTED READINGS

Bauckham, Richard. *Jesus and the Eyewitnesses: The Gospels as Eyewitness Testimony*. Grand Rapids: William B. Eerdmans, 2006.

Benedict XVI. "The Ministry and Life of Priests." October 24, 1995. In *The Essential Pope Benedict XVI*, edited by John F. Thorton and Susan B. Varenne, 305-318. New York: Harper Collins, 2007.

_____. Homilies and Reflections delivered during the 12th Ordinary General Assembly of Bishops (Synod on Scripture). http://www.vatican.va/roman_curia/synod/.

Bradshaw, Paul. *Daily Prayer in the early Church: A Study of the Origins and Early Development of the Divine Office*. New York: Oxford University Press, 1982.

Burghardt, Walter J. *Preaching: The Art and the Craft*. New York: Paulist Press, 1987.

Hahn, Scott W. *Covenant and Communion: The Biblical Theology of Pope Benedict XVI*. Grand Rapids, MI: Brazos Press, 2009.

Studzinski, Raymond. *Reading to Live: The Evolving Practice of Lectio Divina*. Collegeville: Cistercian Publications, 2009.

Untener, Ken. *Preaching Better: Practical Suggestions for Homilists*. New York: Paulist Press, 1999.

Wister, Robert J., ed. *Priests: Identity and Ministry*. Wilmington: Michael Glazier, 1990.

Wright, N. T. *The Challenge of Jesus: Rediscovering Who Jesus Was and Is*. Downer Grove: Intervarsity Press, 1999.

Chapter Three

MEN OF FAITH:
PRIESTS AND CHURCH TEACHING

Rev. Robert A. Pesarchick, S.T.D.

In his *1986 Holy Thursday Letter to Priests,* Pope John Paul II stated:

> Dear brother priests, you are deeply convinced of the importance of proclaiming the Gospel, which the Second Vatican Council placed in the first rank of the functions of a priest. You seek through catechesis, through preaching and in other forms which also include the media, to touch the hearts of our contemporaries, with their hopes and uncertainties, in order to awaken and foster faith.[1]

One of the central aspects of the exercise of the ministry and mission of the ministerial priesthood is that of proclaiming the Gospel through teaching and explaining the deposit of the Church's faith. In this reflection we will examine the role, or ministry, of the priest as teacher. Primarily, but not exclusively, priests exercise their role as teachers of the faith through preaching and catechesis.

Priests have as their model and patron in carrying out this ministry the Curé of Ars, Saint John Vianney. In his letter of proclamation for the Year for Priests, Pope Benedict XVI indicated this: "The Curé devoted himself completely to his parish's conversion, setting before

---

[1] John Paul II, 1986 Holy Thursday Letter, no. 9, *Holy Thursday Letters: To My Brother Priests,* James P. Socias, ed. (Chicago: Midwest Theological Forum, 1992), 167.

all else the Christian education of the people in his care."[2] Saint John, despite the difficulties he experienced in his seminary studies, spent long hours in study preparing his homilies and the catecheses he used for his parishioners both young and old. In this regard Pope John Paul II in the Letter cited above wrote:

> The Curé of Ars was also careful never to neglect in any way the ministry of the Word, which is absolutely necessary in predisposing people to faith and conversion ... We know how long he spent, especially at the beginning, in laboriously composing his Sunday sermons ... His catechetical instructions to the children also formed an important part of his ministry, and the adults gladly joined the children so as to profit from this matchless testimony which flowed from his heart.[3]

In his role as teacher, in the same manner as all who catechize, the ministerial priest

> must constantly endeavor to transmit by his teaching and behavior the teaching and life of Jesus. He will not seek to keep directed towards himself and his personal opinions the attention and the consent of the mind and heart of the person he is catechizing .... he will not try to inculcate his personal opinions and options as if they expressed Christ's teaching and the lessons of His life.[4]

In order to do this the priest must then look upon himself as a "man of the Church" possessing an *anima ecclesiastica,* always thinking with the mind and intentions of the Church. Rather than presenting his own ideas and theories or those of theologians, the priest must endeavor to preach and teach as the faith and doctrine of the Church only that which has been put forward by the teaching office

---

[2] Letter of His Holiness Pope Benedict XVI Proclaiming a Year for Priests on the 150th Anniversary of the *Dies Natalis* of the Curé of Ars, accessed May 7, 2010, http://www.vatican.va/holy_father/benedict_ xvi/ letters/2009/documents/hf_ben-xvi_let_20090616_anno-sacerdotale_ en.html.

[3] John Paul II, 1986 Holy Thursday Letter, no. 9, *Holy Thursday Letters*, 166-67.

[4] Pope John Paul II, *Catechesi Tradendae*, no. 6.

of the Church, the *Magisterium* of the pope and bishops, as the faith and doctrine of the Catholic Church. To be true to their mission as authentic teachers of the Church's faith and doctrine, priests must know and study the teaching of the Church and strive to explain and present it publicly in a clear and integral manner.

Pope John Paul II stated in *Pastores Dabo Vobis:*

> [I]n order that he himself may possess and give to the faithful the guarantee that he is transmitting the Gospel in its fullness, the priest is called to develop a special sensitivity, love and docility to the living tradition of the Church and to her *Magisterium.* These are not foreign to the word, but serve its proper interpretation and preserve its authentic meaning.[5]

Obviously, one certain way to do this is to read and study the great compendium of the authentic faith and doctrine of the Church, the *Catechism of the Catholic Church.* As the *Directory on the Ministry and Life of Priests* states: "To such end, the priest has the Catechism of the Catholic Church as his principle point of reference. This text, in fact, contains the sound and authentic norm of the teaching of the Church."[6] However, as men of the Church striving to know and assimilate her teaching, it is also necessary that priests understand the nature of the *Magisterium* of the Church, how it is exercised by the pope and bishops and the various levels of magisterial teaching which are found throughout the *Catechism.*[7] Prior to considering these topics it is important to reflect on the magisterial or teaching

---

[5] Pope John Paul II, *Pastores Dabo Vobis,* no. 26.

[6] Congregation for the Clergy, *Directory on the Ministry and Life of Priests,* no. 47.

[7] Cf. Joseph Cardinal Ratzinger, "Worthiness to Receive Holy Communion—General Principles," Letter July 9, 2004, accessed May 8, 2010, http://www.catholicculture.org/culture/library/view.cfm?recnum=6041: "Not all moral issues have the same moral weight as abortion and euthanasia. For example, if a Catholic were to be at odds with the Holy Father on the application of capital punishment or on the decision to wage war, he would not for that reason be considered unworthy to present himself to receive Holy Communion. While the Church exhorts civil authorities to seek peace, not war, and to exercise discretion and mercy in imposing punishment on criminals, it may still be permissible to take up arms to repel an aggressor or to have recourse to capital punishment. There may be a legitimate diversity

function of the apostolic mission and ministry of the bishops and to what extent and how priests participate in this function in their pastoral ministry as teachers.

THE APOSTOLIC MISSION AND MINISTRY

In the years prior to the Second Vatican Council, Pius XII in the encyclical *Mystici Corporis Christi* (1943) affirmed the traditional teaching that the bishops are "by divine institution the successors of the Apostles."[8] The Second Vatican Council reaffirmed this teaching in the Dogmatic Constitution on the Church, *Lumen Gentium:* "The sacred council teaches that bishops by divine institution have succeeded to the place of the Apostles as shepherds of the Church."[9] As successors to the place of the Apostles through sacramental ordination, bishops are given the powers and duties necessary for the apostolic ministry through which Christ makes Himself present to the Church, as the council states in *Lumen Gentium:*

> In the bishops, therefore, for whom priests are assistants, Our Lord Jesus Christ, the Supreme High Priest, is present in the midst of those who believe. For sitting at the right hand of God the Father, He is not absent from the gathering of His high priests, but above all through their excellent service He is preaching the word of God to all nations, and constantly administering the sacraments of faith to those who believe, by their paternal functioning He incorporates new members in His Body by a heavenly regeneration, and finally by their wisdom and prudence He directs and guides the People of the New Testament in their pilgrimage toward eternal happiness. These pastors, chosen to shepherd the Lord's flock of the elect, are servants of Christ and stewards of the mysteries of God, to whom has been assigned the bearing of witness to the

---

of opinion even among Catholics about waging war and applying the death penalty, but not however with regard to abortion and euthanasia."

[8] Cf. Denzinger-Schönmetzer, *Enchiridion Symbolorum Definitionum et Declarationem* (Rome: Herder, 1964), 3804. Hereafter DS.

[9] Second Vatican Council, *Lumen Gentium*, no. 21.

Gospel of the grace of God, and the ministration of the Spirit and of justice in glory.[10]

Directly connected to the teaching of the council on the bishops as successors to the place of the Apostles by divine institution *(ex divina institutione)* is the teaching of the council in *Lumen Gentium* on the sacramental nature of the episcopate, i.e., episcopal consecration is sacramental ordination and not simply the conferral of jurisdiction to teach, govern and sanctify:

> For the discharging of such great duties, the apostles were enriched by Christ with a special outpouring of the Holy Spirit coming upon them, and they passed on this spiritual gift to their helpers by the imposition of hands, and it has been transmitted down to us in episcopal consecration. And the Sacred Council teaches that by episcopal consecration the fullness of the sacrament of Orders is conferred, that fullness of power, namely, which both in the Church's liturgical practice and in the language of the Fathers of the Church is called the high priesthood, the supreme power of the sacred ministry. But episcopal consecration, together with the office of sanctifying, also confers the office of teaching and of governing, which, however, of its very nature, can be exercised only in hierarchical communion with the head and the members of the college. For from the tradition, which is expressed especially in liturgical rites and in the practice of both the Church of the East and of the West, it is clear that, by means of the imposition of hands and the words of consecration, the grace of the Holy Spirit is so conferred, and the sacred character so impressed, that bishops in an eminent and visible way sustain the roles of Christ Himself as Teacher, Shepherd and High Priest, and that they act in His person.[11]

This means that bishops receive in sacramental ordination participation in the mission given by Jesus to the Apostles. Bishops receive a sacred character and mission to teach, sanctify and govern

---

[10] Ibid.

[11] Ibid.

the Church with the authority of Christ and to act in His person. Here we are considering the aspect of their mission to sustain and make visible the role of Christ as teacher, who in His person offers to the world the fullness of Divine Revelation. Their teaching, then, is in service to the Word of God and the proclamation of the Gospel. This is one of their primary duties as indicated by the Second Vatican Council:

> Among the principal duties of bishops the preaching of the Gospel occupies an eminent place. For bishops are preachers of the faith, who lead new disciples to Christ, and they are authentic teachers, that is, teachers endowed with the authority of Christ, who preach to the people committed to them the faith they must believe and put into practice, and by the light of the Holy Spirit illustrate that faith. They bring forth from the treasury of revelation new things and old (cf. Mt 13:52), making it bear fruit and vigilantly warding off any errors that threaten their flock (cf. 2 Tm 4:1-4). Bishops, teaching in communion with the Roman Pontiff, are to be respected by all as witnesses to divine and Catholic truth. In matters of faith and morals, the bishops speak in the name of Christ and the faithful are to accept their teaching and adhere to it with a religious assent.[12]

In exercising their role, or office of teaching, the pope and bishops under the direction and inspiration of the Holy Spirit—the "Spirit of Truth" (Jn 14:17)—are to listen to and reflect upon the teaching of Christ. They are also to penetrate more profoundly His message so that its fullness and richness may be grasped and salvation be offered to all mankind. This authoritative teaching is said to be an exercise of the Church's *Magisterium*. The teaching includes the truths entrusted to the Church by Christ for the sake of our salvation by the Church's pastors.

The pope and bishops in communion with him are called the *Magisterium* of the Church, or the "teaching office" of the Church.

---

[12] Second Vatican Council, *Lumen Gentium*, no. 25; cf. also the Council's Decree on the Pastoral Office of Bishops in the Church, *Christus Dominus*, nos. 2, 12-14.

It is important to consider the meaning of the term *Magisterium* in itself and as it is used by the Church in her teaching and practice.

WHAT IS THE MAGISTERIUM?[13]

The Concept of Magisterium. Etymologically the word *Magisterium* has its roots in the Latin word *magister*. *Magister* is rooted in the word *magis* and had a connotation of authority. It corresponded to our English word "master," not only in the sense of a schoolmaster but in the broader sense of master, as a person is master of servants or employees, or a trade or of a ship. More and more it came to be commonly used for a teacher, and *Magisterium* came more and more to be identified with the role and authority of some aspect of teaching. Nonetheless, even in late Latin, it still maintained its broader notion of other functions and roles which connoted authority of various kinds. Our English word "magistrate" is an example of a broader notion of the term.

The foundation of the Church's *Magisterium* in the New Testament writings is quite clear. Based on New Testament evidence one can affirm that the Apostles received from Christ the mandate to teach in His name. Since Jesus left nothing in writing, the entire Christian message and faith rests entirely on the witness of the disciples of Jesus, especially on the twelve selected from the larger band of believers. Being a Christian means to be one who "believes in me (Christ) through their word" (Jn 17:20). Apart from the apostolic testimony we would know nothing specifically of what Christ said or did. In Mk 3:14, Jesus selects twelve men "that they might be with him and he might send them forth to preach." Later in Mk 16:15 they are sent out by the risen Jesus to "proclaim the good news to the whole creation." At the conclusion of the Gospel of Matthew, Jesus tells them to go out and "make disciples of all nations . . . teaching them to observe everything that I have commanded you" (Mt 28:19-20). Earlier in the same Gospel, Jesus not only gives them His mandate to teach but gives them His own authority, identifying

---

[13] For sources on this matter see Avery Dulles, *Magisterium* (Naples, FL: Sapientia Press, 2007), 11-20 and 21-34; Aidan Nichols, *The Shape of Catholic Theology* (Edinburgh: T&T Clark, 1991), 248-260; Jared Wicks, *Doing Theology* (Mahwah: Paulist Press, 2009), 92-105.

Himself with them: "Whoever receives you receives me, and whoever receives me receives the one who sent me " (Mt 10:40).

Based on New Testament evidence, one can also affirm that the Apostles commissioned by Christ to teach in His name shared this mission with co-workers they enlisted in the same pastoral ministry after the Resurrection and Ascension of Jesus. This is evident in the Acts of the Apostles; e.g., the address of Saint Paul to the elders, or *episcopoi,* of the Church of Ephesus (20:17-35). In verses 28-31 he alerts them that they are to be attentive to the purity of doctrine, and in confronting those who would spread false teaching they are to speak out with their authority if necessary. It is evident that these elders (overseers) share in the mandate and authority of the Apostle Paul, a mandate and authority given him by the Risen Jesus. This again becomes most evident in the Pastoral Epistles attributed to Saint Paul, i.e. 1-2 Timothy and Titus. In these letters both Timothy and Titus are constantly reminded of their mission as teachers; e.g., Timothy is told: "Command and teach these things" (1 Tm 4:11); and "Until I arrive, attend to the reading, exhortation, and teaching (1 Tm 4:13); and further: "Attend to yourself and to your teaching." (1 Tm 4:16); and finally: "[B]e persistent whether it is convenient or inconvenient; convince, reprimand, encourage through all patience and teaching" (2 Tm 4:2). In Titus a similar exhortation is given: "As for yourself, you must say what is consistent with sound doctrine" (Ti 2:1). Thus, it is quite clear based on these few New Testament citations (to which countless others could be added) that the Apostles shared with others the mandate given them by Christ to teach in His name.

Present in the New Testament is not only the collaboration of the Apostles with others to share in their teaching mandate, but also the principle of succession in regard to the commission to teach. In the Acts of the Apostles, where Saint Paul addresses the elders of the Church at Ephesus, he envisions a time after his own death and warns them: "savage wolves will come in among you" in which case it will be the task of those whom "the Holy Spirit has made *episcopoi*" to be alert to safeguard the flock from corruption by those who are "speaking perverse things" (Acts 20:28-31). This is also evident in the Pastoral Epistles. In 2 Tm 4:1-8, Timothy is instructed to carry on this ministry after the death of Saint Paul. Timothy is forewarned to choose men who are fitting teachers for the role of *episcopos* in the community. In 2 Tm 2:2, Timothy is exhorted: "And what you heard from me through many witnesses entrust to faithful people who will have the ability to teach others as well." In like manner, Titus is instructed that the choice of elder must hold fast "to the true message as taught so that he will be able both to exhort with sound doctrine and to refute opponents (Ti 1:9). It becomes quite clear based on this small example of New Testament evidence (many more texts could be cited) that there is a strict association between the ministry of pastoral leadership (leading and sanctifying) and the ministry of teaching in the New Testament Church, exercised by those appointed leaders in the Church community. This union of the two ministries (threefold *munera*, or office in later Church teaching—to teach, lead and sanctify, see *Lumen Gentium* no. 21) in the same person will be passed over into the post-apostolic Church, and then down to our own time both in the Eastern and the Western Church.

In the terminology of medieval Scholasticism, *Magisterium* came to mean the authority of someone who teaches. The symbol of teaching authority was seen to be the *cathedra,* or chair. Saint Thomas spoke of two such chairs of authority or *Magisterium:* the *Magisterium cathedrae pastoralis* of the bishop and the *Magisterium cathedrae magistralis* of the university theologian. Both were seen to embody an authority, however of a different type. The bishop's authority is seen as rooted in his role as head of the local Church, following from his union with the college of bishops which succeeds the Apostolic College in a certain sense. The theologian's authority is seen to reside in his knowledge or expertise over the subject matter of theology.

In recent Church history, from the time of Gregory XVI (1831-1846) who first used the term *Magisterium* to describe the teaching office of the papacy in an official document, his encyclical *Commissum Divinitus* (1835), to the present, the term has come to be used exclusively for the teaching office of the pope and bishops. While the teaching role of theologians is not being denied, in technical terminology *Magisterium* now ordinarily refers to the teaching role of the bishops of the Church. It has come to be used almost exclusively in theology and Church documents to designate the teaching function of the hierarchy, and the hierarchy itself, as the bearers of this function or office of authoritative teaching. In the First Vatican Council's (1870) document on Divine Revelation and Faith, *Dei Filius*, it refers to the teaching of doctrine by the Church, either by a solemn judgment or by its ordinary and universal teaching authority (*sive solemni iudicio sive ordinario et universali magisterio*)—the pope and the bishops in communion with him and the Roman Church.

Again Vatican I, in its decree of July 18, 1870, *Pastor Aeternus*, which concerned the papal primacy, speaks of the pope exercising the supreme power of *Magisterium*. Even the chapter of the decree, which defined papal infallibility, is entitled "On the infallible *Magisterium* of the Roman Pontiff." At the Second Vatican Council (1962-1965), *Magisterium* is used in an almost exclusive way to designate the pastoral teaching office of the hierarchy. *Lumen Gentium* no. 18 speaks of the infallible *Magisterium* of the Roman Pontiff; no. 22 speaks of the order of bishops as the successor to the College of Apostles as teachers (i.e., *Magisterium*); no. 25 treats of the authentic and supreme *Magisterium* of the Roman Pontiff. The same section then goes on to speak of the bishops gathered in an Ecumenical council as exercising supreme *Magisterium* with the Roman Pontiff as successor of the Apostle Peter. Again, in the Dogmatic Constitution on Divine Revelation, *Dei Verbum*, the task of the hierarchical *Magisterium* is described as follows:

> But the task of authentically interpreting the word of God, whether written or handed on, (8) has been entrusted exclusively to the living teaching office of the Church, (9) whose authority is exercised in the name of Jesus Christ. This teaching office is not above the word of God, but serves it, teaching only what has been handed on, listening to it devoutly, guarding it scrupulously and explaining it faithfully in accord with a divine commission and with the help of the Holy Spirit, it draws from this one deposit of faith everything which it presents for belief as divinely revealed.[14]

Here the *Magisterium* is said to be the authentic (*authentice*), i.e., authoritative interpreter of the Word of God. And in *Lumen Gentium*, no. 25, the pope and bishops are said to be authentic: authoritative teachers. In stating this, the council is not saying that the only genuine teachers are the pope and bishops, or that the only genuine interpretation of the Word of God in Sacred Scripture and

---

[14] Second Vatican Council, *Dei Verbum*, no. 10.

Tradition is that given by the hierarchical *Magisterium*.[15] Rather the Latin words *authenticum* and *authentice* used in these and other passages to describe the *Magisterium* of the pope and bishops means authoritative (once in older English the word authentic also had the connotation of authority but in modern usage has come to be used exclusively with the meaning "genuine"). So what is being stated here is that the hierarchical *Magisterium* teaches with the authority given it by Christ as successor to the Apostolic College—Peter and the twelve Apostles. This means that the bishops receive their teaching authority by virtue of inheriting from the Apostles the mandate to teach in Christ's own name—they receive this directly from Christ with the conferral of ordination to the episcopate through Apostolic Succession.

THE PARTICIPATION OF PRESBYTERS IN THE APOSTOLIC MISSION AND THE MINISTRY OF PRIESTS

The Second Vatican Council takes up the nature of the priesthood in *Lumen Gentium* no. 28 and then further developed in the Decree on the Ministry and Life of priests, *Presbyterorum Ordinis* no. 2. *Lumen Gentium* describes the nature of the priesthood as follows:

> Christ, whom the Father has sanctified and sent into the world, has through His apostles, made their successors, the bishops, partakers of His consecration and His mission. They have legitimately handed on to different individuals in the Church various degrees of participation in this ministry. Thus the divinely established ecclesiastical ministry is exercised on different levels by those who from antiquity have been called bishops, priests and deacons. Priests, although they do not possess the highest degree of the priesthood, and although they are dependent on the bishops in the exercise of their power, nevertheless are united with the bishops in sacerdotal dignity. By the power of the sacrament of Orders, in the image of Christ

---

[15] Cf. René Latourelle, *Theology of Revelation* (New York: Alba House, 1987), 482ff.

the eternal high Priest, they are consecrated to preach the Gospel and shepherd the faithful and to celebrate divine worship, so that they are true priests of the New Testament.[16]

Similarly the nature of the priesthood is developed in *Presbyterorum Ordinis* in the following way:

Therefore, having sent the apostles just as he himself been sent by the Father, Christ, through the apostles themselves, made their successors, the bishops sharers in his consecration and mission. The office of their ministry has been handed down, in a lesser degree indeed, to the priests. Established in the order of the priesthood they can be co-workers of the episcopal order for the proper fulfillment of the apostolic mission entrusted to priests by Christ.

The office of priests, since it is connected with the episcopal order, also, in its own degree, shares the authority by which Christ builds up, sanctifies and rules His Body. Wherefore the priesthood, while indeed it presupposes the sacraments of Christian initiation, is conferred by that special sacrament; through it priests, by the anointing of the Holy Spirit, are signed with a special character and are conformed to Christ the Priest in such a way that they can act in the person of Christ the Head.[17]

The essence of the ministerial priesthood present in both the episcopal and presbyteral degrees of the sacrament of Order is to represent [in the sense of Christ, the high priest, making Himself present to His Church through the ministerial priesthood] Christ as Head and Spouse of the Church, His Body and Bride. While there is an ontological unity to the sacrament of Orders [the three degrees are of one sacrament], it is only in the episcopal and presbyteral degrees that those ordained participate in the ministerial priesthood of Christ and are consecrated to represent Him as Head and Spouse. While they do not participate in the fullness of the ministerial priesthood as do the bishops, the presbyteral degree is a true sharing in the ministerial priesthood of Christ. They are "configured' to Christ, the Head and

---

[16] Second Vatican Council, *Lumen Gentium*, no. 28.

[17] Second Vatican Council, *Presbyterorum Ordinis*, no. 2.

Spouse of the Church, by ordination in such a way that they can act in the person of Christ the Head. This means that ministerial priests, through the consecration of the sacrament of Orders, receive from the person of Christ Himself and the working of the Holy Spirit a true participation in the consecration and saving mission of Christ as high priest and head of the Church.

The functions of those who receive the second degree of the sacrament of Orders are indicated in *Lumen Gentium* no. 28 and then developed in chapter 2 of *Presbyterorum Ordinis:*

> By the power of the sacrament of Orders, in the image of Christ the eternal high Priest, they are consecrated to preach the Gospel and shepherd the faithful and to celebrate divine worship, so that they are true priests of the New Testament. Partakers of the function of Christ the sole Mediator, on their level of ministry, they announce the divine word to all. They exercise their sacred function especially in the Eucharistic worship or the celebration of the Mass, by which, acting in the person of Christ and proclaiming His Mystery, they unite the prayers of the faithful with the sacrifice of their Head and renew and apply in the sacrifice of the Mass until the coming of the Lord the only sacrifice of the New Testament, namely that of Christ offering Himself once for all a spotless Victim to the Father. For the sick and the sinners among the faithful, they exercise the ministry of alleviation and reconciliation and they present the needs and the prayers of the faithful to God the Father. Exercising within the limits of their authority the function of Christ as Shepherd and Head, they gather together God's family as a brotherhood all of one mind, and lead them in the Spirit, through Christ, to God the Father. In the midst of the flock they adore Him in spirit and in truth. Finally, they labor in word and doctrine, believing what they have read and meditated upon in the law of God, teaching what they have believed, and putting in practice in their own lives what they have taught.[18]

---

[18] Second Vatican Council, *Lumen Gentium*, no. 28.

As cooperators or collaborators with the bishops in the apostolic mission received from Christ, priests also exercise the ministerial functions of proclamation of the Word, of sanctifying and of governing in the name of Christ as they participate in His work as the one, unique Mediator.[19] As was indicated above in the apostolic mission and ministry of the pope and college of bishops, the dimension of proclaiming the Word of God involves teaching the Church through the exercise of the *Magisterium*. One can then conclude that priests in a dependent manner participate in the *Magisterium* of the pope and bishops by virtue of their sharing in the apostolic mission and ministry of the bishops.

While priests do not directly exercise a *Magisterium* in the sense of the bishops who teach the Church in the name of Christ, they do in the teaching of the faithful entrusted to their care represent the *Magisterium* of the bishops and so must present to the faithful the official magisterial teaching of the Church. In treating the mission of priests as "heralds and transmitters of the faith," the *Directory on the Ministry and Life of Priests* states: "Such ministry, developed within the hierarchical community, enables him to authoritatively express the Catholic faith and give official testimony of the faith of the Church."[20] The Directory goes on to state that "the priest will wisely avoid falsifying, reducing, distorting or diluting the content of the divine message."[21] Certainly one way in which priests can access and know the authentic teaching of the *Magisterium* is to turn to the *Catechism of the Catholic Church*, for as the Directory indicates: "this text, in fact, contains the sound and authentic norm of the teaching of the Church."

While this is obligatory for priests to exercise their ministry of teaching the faithful, it is also helpful for priests to be familiar with and to understand the various forms the *Magisterium* of the pope and bishops can take, the various levels of magisterial teaching, and the various degrees of obedient response owed to this teaching on the part of all the faithful. Before examining the forms and levels of magisterial teaching [which are contained in the *CCC*] and the response

---

[19] See Second Vatican Council, *Presbyterorum Ordinis*, nos. 4-6.

[20] Congregation for the Clergy, *Directory on the Ministry and Life of Priests*, no. 45.

[21] Ibid.

of the faithful, it is necessary first to have a proper understanding of the Church's teaching regarding the gift, or charism of infallibility and the *Magisterium* of the pope and bishops.

THE CHARISM OF INFALLIBILITY AND THE MAGISTERIUM OF THE CHURCH[22]

In the first place, it is important to make a fundamental distinction between the mark of the indefectibility of the entire Church, and the charism of infallibility that is one of the ways the risen Jesus through the Holy Spirit guarantees the fundamental indefectibility of His Body and Bride, the Church.[23] The indefectibility of the Church does not mean that the Church, in its pilgrimage of faith, is totally perfect or without need of reform. What it signifies is that in fundamental, essential matters of faith and Christian life that are necessary for salvation, the Church as guided by the Holy Spirit promised by Christ cannot err. In the letter to the Ephesians, Saint Paul states that "Christ loved the church and handed himself over for her" (Eph 5:25). If so, how could He allow her to become essentially corrupt and therefore lost to Him? It is a matter of confidence in divine providence and not in human powers. The Second Vatican Council states in *Lumen Gentium*:

> Moving forward through trial and tribulation, the Church is strengthened by the power of God's grace, which was promised to her by the Lord, so that in the weakness of the flesh she may not waver from perfect fidelity, but remain a bride worthy of her Lord, and moved by the Holy Spirit may never cease to renew herself, until through the Cross she arrives at the light which knows no setting.[24]

---

[22] Cf. Avery Dulles, *Magisterium*, 59-65.

[23] On this distinction see James T. O'Connor, *The Gift of Infallibility* (San Francisco: Ignatius Press, 2008), 105-109 and Ludwig Ott, *Fundamentals of Catholic Dogma* (Rockford, IL: Tan Books and Publishers, Inc., 1974), 296-298.

[24] Second Vatican Council, *Lumen Gentium*, no. 9.

Though in need of reform due to human weakness and sin, in essential matters pertaining to man's salvation the Church possesses indefectibility.[25]

The charism of infallibility is given to the Church as a means of keeping the Church indefectible in essential matters concerning human salvation. This concept is clearly rooted in the New Testament itself which envisions this infallibility to be possessed by the Church community as a whole. In 1 Tm 3:15, the Church is described as the "pillar and foundation of the truth." Thus, it is an allusion to the apostolic assurance that the Church has a permanence in the truth revealed by Christ. This conviction is further supported by the promise of Jesus explicitly given in the Farewell Discourse in the Gospel of John that he would send the Spirit of all truth: "... I will ask the Father, and he will give you another Advocate to be with you always, the Spirit of Truth ..." (Jn 14:16-17). Again, in Jn 15:26, "When the Advocate comes whom I will send you from the Father, the Spirit of truth that proceeds from the Father, he will testify to me." In Jn 16:13, Jesus says, "But when he comes, the Spirit of truth, he will guide you to all truth. He will not speak on his own, but he will speak what he hears, and will declare to you the things that are coming." This ecclesial infallibility is witnessed to again and further specified in Mt 16:18, when Jesus says to Peter, "... upon this rock I will build my church, and the gates of the netherworld shall not prevail against it." Then His promise in Matthew 28:20: "And behold, I am with you always, until the end of the age." These passages, among a host of others, express the conviction of the apostolic Church that the presence of Christ in the Spirit to the Church would confirm her in truth and keep her from essential error.

This notion of the infallibility of the entire Church is concisely summed up in *Lumen Gentium*:

> The holy people of God shares also in Christ's prophetic office; it spreads abroad a living witness to Him, especially by means of a life of faith and charity and by offering to God a sacrifice of praise, the tribute of lips which give praise to His name. The entire body of the faithful, anointed as they are by the Holy One, cannot err in

---

[25] Cf. also *Catechism of the Catholic Church*, no. 824 and *Unitatis Redintegratio*, no. 3, par. 5.

matters of belief. They manifest this special property by means of the whole peoples' supernatural discernment in matters of faith when "from the Bishops down to the last of the lay faithful" they show universal agreement in matters of faith and morals. That discernment in matters of faith is aroused and sustained by the Spirit of truth. It is exercised under the guidance of the sacred teaching authority, in faithful and respectful obedience to which the people of God accepts that which is not just the word of men but truly the word of God. Through it, the people of God adheres unwaveringly to the faith given once and for all to the saints, penetrates it more deeply with right thinking, and applies it more fully in its life.[26]

THE SUBJECT AND OBJECT OF THE INFALLIBILITY OF THE CHURCH

The Infallibility of the Magisterium.[27] We need now to consider who is the subject of the infallibility of the Church, which is brought about by the continued presence and activity of Christ in His Spirit. This subject is the bearer of the charism given by the Holy Spirit. A three-fold division can be made based on the teaching of the Second Vatican Council in *Lumen Gentium* nos. 12 and 25.

1. It is clear from *Lumen Gentium* no. 12 that the primary subject of the charism of infallibility is the entire people of God, or the Church as a whole. In this text the people of God as a whole is described as the addressee and the bearer of the truth of the Word of God revealed in and through the person of Christ. The infallibility of the believed and lived truth of revelation is then anchored in the people of God as a whole; however, always keeping in mind that the Church, or the people of God, is a hierarchically structured reality of ministries and charisms. Individuals only can recognize and fulfill their role as proclaimers of truth in dependence upon and in service to the whole Church.

---

[26] Second Vatican Council, *Lumen Gentium*, no. 12.

[27] For sources on this see J. O'Connor, *The Gift of Infallibility*, 100-137 and A. Dulles, *Magisterium*, 65-81.

2. Given the hierarchical structure of the Church there exist certain ministries, which in a special way are called to lead and to proclaim the truth of revelation. This applies in particular to the body of bishops as a whole, which succeeds to the apostolic authority of leading and teaching in the name of Christ. *Lumen Gentium* states:

> For bishops are preachers of the faith, who lead new disciples to Christ, and *they are authentic teachers, that is, teachers endowed with the authority of Christ,* who preach to the people committed to them the faith they must believe and put into practice, and by the light of the Holy Spirit illustrate that faith[28] (italics added).

Thus, under certain circumstances in determining matters of faith and morals to be believed by the entire Church, the body of bishops in union with their head, the bishop of Rome, the pope, shares in a particular way the charism of infallibility. When and how they become the subject or bearer of this charism is explained by *Lumen Gentium*:

> Although the individual bishops do not enjoy the prerogative of infallibility, they nevertheless proclaim Christ's doctrine infallibly whenever, even though dispersed through the world, but still maintaining the bond of communion among themselves and with the successor of Peter, and authentically teaching matters of faith and morals, they are in agreement on one position as definitively to be held. This is even more clearly verified when, gathered together in an ecumenical council, they are teachers and judges of faith and morals for the universal Church, whose definitions must be adhered to with the submission of faith.[29]

It is clear from this passage that although the individual bishops do not share in the charism of ecclesial infallibility, there are occasions and circumstances that, as a body—episcopal college—in union with the successor of Peter, the bishop of Rome, they do share

---

[28] Second Vatican Council, *Lumen Gentium*, no. 25.

[29] Ibid.

in this charism as they make determinations of the contents of the faith binding on all believers. The Council cites two such occasions:

A) Ordinary and Universal *Magisterium*—When dispersed throughout the world, but still in union with the pope, they teach with the authority of Christ, a matter concerning faith or morals which they judge in agreement must be definitively held by all the faithful. In exercising this *Magisterium*, they proclaim the teaching and are protected by the charism of infallibility.

B) Gathered together in an Ecumenical Council acting as both teachers and judges of faith and morals, they determine or define a teaching to be held definitively by the entire Church. In this they enjoy the charism of infallibility.

3. The final, supreme subject or bearer of this ecclesial infallibility is the pope: he is the head of the college of bishops, the Church's supreme pastor, the successor of Peter, and the bishop of Rome. On this *Lumen Gentium* states:

> And this infallibility with which the Divine Redeemer willed His Church to be endowed in defining doctrine of faith and morals, extends as far as the deposit of Revelation extends, which must be religiously guarded and faithfully expounded. And this is the infallibility which the Roman Pontiff, the head of the college of bishops, enjoys in virtue of his office, when, as the supreme shepherd and teacher of all the faithful, who confirms his brethren in their faith, by a definitive act he proclaims a doctrine of faith or morals. And therefore his definitions, of themselves, and not from the consent of the Church, are justly styled irreformable, since they are pronounced with the assistance of the Holy Spirit, promised to him in blessed Peter, and therefore they need no approval of others, nor do they allow an appeal to any other judgment. For then the Roman Pontiff is not pronouncing judgment as a private person, but as the supreme teacher of the universal Church, in whom the charism of infallibility of the Church itself is individually present, he is expounding or defending a doctrine of Catholic faith. The infallibility promised to the Church resides also in the body of Bishops, when that body exercises the supreme *Magisterium* with the

successor of Peter. To these definitions the assent of the Church can never be wanting, on account of the activity of that same Holy Spirit, by which the whole flock of Christ is preserved and progresses in unity of faith.[30]

Here the pope acting in virtue of his office as supreme pastor and teacher of all the faithful (called upon by Christ to confirm his brethren in the faith, Lk. 22:31-32) declares in an absolute decision or determination a matter concerning faith or morals. These decisions or definitions are irreformable of themselves and do not depend on the consent of the Church, for they are guided by the Holy Spirit. In doing this the pope is not acting as a private person, but as the supreme teacher (*Magisterium*) of the universal Church in whom the Church's own charism exists individually when he determines definitively a teaching of faith or morals for the entire Church. In such a declaration the pope is said to be speaking *ex cathedra* (i.e. from his office as universal shepherd of the entire Church).[31]

We now turn to the object of the charism of magisterial infallibility of both the pope and the body of bishops in union with him. The teaching of the Church is clear about the conditions and the scope of when this charism of the Holy Spirit comes into play in magisterial teachings or declarations. Not just any teaching of the pope and the body of bishops can be said to be protected by this charism. The teaching must be in regard to revealed matters of faith or morals intrinsically connected to revealed truths.

The object of the infallible *Magisterium* is ordinarily divided into a primary and secondary object based on the wording of the First and Second Vatican Councils' teaching, as well as the interpretations offered by the theological commissions in the *Acta* of the councils.

The Primary Object: The deposit of faith, i.e. revelation as contained or passed on in Sacred Scripture and Tradition. This is usually expressed by the statement, "matters regarding faith and morals,"

---

[30] Ibid. In this the Council is reiterating, now in the wider perspective of the episcopal college, the teaching of Vatican I in its decree of July 18, 1870, *Pastor Aeternus,* which defined Papal Infallibility (DS 3074) as a divinely revealed dogma.

[31] For example, *Benedictus Deus,* AD 1336 (DS 1000-1001); *Ineffabilis Deus,* AD 1854 (DS 2800-2804); *Munificentissimus Deus,* AD 1950 (DS 3900-3904).

i.e., revealed facts necessary for our salvation. In this, as *Dei Verbum* states, "we now await no further new public revelation"[32] before the Parousia, i.e., no new facts will be added to the deposit of faith.

The Secondary Object: These are all those truths not strictly revealed by God and contained in the deposit of faith but which are necessary to be held as true in order to guard and expound the deposit of faith in its purity and integrity. Thus, these truths are connected intrinsically to the deposit, even if they are not contained in it. This is implied in the wording of the Vatican councils which, when speaking of the pope or the body of bishops in union with him determining definitively a matter to be held by the faithful, use *definitive tenendam,* and not, as was proposed in the conciliar proceedings, *definitive credendam.* This distinction means that the *Magisterium* can teach definitively revealed truths which must be held in faith and truths intrinsically connected to revealed truths that must be held and accepted with definitive assent. Ordinarily theological manuals will cite the following as examples of this secondary object: 1) Theological conclusions—one premise is a directly revealed truth of faith and the second premise is a truth not directly revealed. These conclusions are said to be mediately or virtually revealed (e.g. abortion and euthanasia, see *Evangelium Vitae* nos. 62 and 65); 2) Dogmatic facts—historical facts not directly revealed but are intrinsically connected with revealed truth (e.g. the Roman episcopate of Saint Peter, the legitimacy of a pope or an Ecumenical council, a canonization[33]); 3) Truths of Reason—not directly revealed but intrinsically connected with revealed truth. Here these philosophical truths are presupposed by the truths of faith which could not be affirmed without them (e.g. the capacity of man to know the truth, man's free will, the natural law). In these cases, these truths can be definitively taught by the *Magisterium* of the pope or the body of bishops in union with him; and if the conditions are met[34] this teaching can enjoy the protection of the Holy Spirit who provides the Church with the charism of infallibility.

---

[32] Second Vatican Council, *Dei Verbum*, no. 4.

[33] Cf. Dulles, *Magisterium*, 78. Here, Dulles disagrees that a canonization is protected by the charism of infallibility.

[34] That is, states that a definition is being given, or that the matter is to be definitively held by the pope, or the body of bishops in union with him

THE EXERCISE OF THE MAGISTERIUM OF THE CHURCH: EXTRAORDINARY AND ORDINARY FORMS

The Extraordinary Form. In solemn pronouncements which determine matters of faith and morals binding on all the faithful and guaranteed by the Holy Spirit through the charism of infallibility, the *Magisterium* is said to exercise an extraordinary function. This can be regarding the pope or the body of bishops in union with the pope.

The first extraordinary use of the *Magisterium* as was cited in *Lumen Gentium* no. 25, is the bishops united with the pope in an Ecumenical council in which they act as teachers and judges of a matter of faith and morals to be determined and held by the entire Church.[35] Here they share in the charism of ecclesial infallibility given by Christ through the Spirit. The second extraordinary use is exercised by the pope alone acting as the supreme pastor and teacher of the universal Church when he proclaims in a definitive act a matter of faith or morals to be held by the entire Church. In this the pope is said, as was seen, to make an *ex cathedra* pronouncement. Here he acts, not as a private person, but as the supreme pastor and teacher, and successor of Peter, in whom the charism of infallibility given to the entire Church exists individually, as he defends, expounds, or determines a matter of faith or morals.

The Ordinary Form. Ordinary and Universal *Magisterium*— Aside from this extraordinary manner of teaching, which is rare, there exists an ordinary, everyday teaching function exercised by the pope and the bishops. This ordinary *Magisterium*, if exercised in a universal manner, in which the body of bishops dispersed throughout the world but in union with the pope agree about a judgment of faith or morals to be definitively held by all the faithful (fulfilling the four conditions of *Lumen Gentium* no. 25) proclaims infallibly the teaching of Christ. Thus, while not exercising the extraordinary

---

in Council or by the ordinary and universal *Magisterium* in an agreement of a matter judged to be held definitively.

[35] For example, the teaching of the council of Nicaea, AD 325, that Jesus is one in substance with the Father; or Vatican I in 1870, in the definition given in *Pastor Aeternus*.

function of *Magisterium* they, the pope and college of bishops, enjoy the protection of the charism of infallibility. However, while the council set conditions for this, it did not specify further any criteria to determine when this was the case.

Pope John Paul II, in certain of his writings, has as head of the college of bishops indicated in a number of instances that certain teachings were proposed definitively by the ordinary and universal *Magisterium*, and this means that the teaching in these cases was protected by the charism of infallibility. Here Pope John Paul made an important contribution in determining when this occurred and the four conditions of *Lumen Gentium* no. 25 have been met. One such example is in the 1994 Apostolic Letter *Ordinatio Sacerdotalis*, where John Paul II stated that the Church has no authority to admit women to priestly ordination and that this decision must be "definitively held" by all the faithful. Joseph Cardinal Ratzinger, then prefect of the Congregation for the Doctrine of the Faith, in an official response to a question about the nature of the pope's teaching in the Apostolic Letter stated: "In this case, an act of the ordinary papal *Magisterium* in itself not infallible, witnesses to the infallibility of the teaching of a doctrine already possessed by the Church."[36] The pope then as head of the college of bishops can formally confirm that on a certain matter the ordinary and universal *Magisterium* has met the conditions of *Lumen Gentium* no. 25 and that they taught the matter in question infallibly.[37] These teaching acts of the ordinary and universal *Magisterium* can be in regard to truths of the primary or secondary object of the *Magisterium* and are called "non-defining" acts to distinguish them from "defining acts" of the extraordinary *Magisterium* of the pope or an ecumenical council.[38]

---

[36] Cf. "Response to the Dubium," *L'Osservatore Romano*, November 22, 1995.

[37] For examples of other such affirmations or confirmations of John Paul II see *Evangelium Vitae*, nos. 57, 62 and 65.

[38] The Congregation for the Doctrine of the Faith in its "Commentary on the Concluding Formula of the 1989 *Professio fidei*" in Dulles' *Magisterium* is quite explicit on this matter: "The *Magisterium* of the Church, however, teaches a doctrine to be believed as divinely revealed (first paragraph) or to be held definitively (second paragraph) with an act which is either defining or non-defining. In the case of a defining act, a truth is solemnly defined by an 'ex cathedra' pronouncement by the Roman Pontiff or by the action of

As we saw in the consideration of the object of the *Magiste-rium* regarding its sharing in the charism of infallibility, its scope is restricted to the deposit of faith or those truths not strictly revealed but that are presupposed by the deposit of faith. This, however, does not exhaust the scope of the *Magisterium* in general. The teaching authority of the Church's pastors includes ordinary teaching on the deposit of faith, disciplinary matters, and even practical judgments which may not be binding beyond the particular time in which they were given. In regard to the latter, these decisions may be based on contingent factors which may change with further investigation; but for the time in which they were pronounced, they were intended to protect and safeguard the faith of the entire Church or to foster the Church's life.[39] Thus, while not enjoying the charism of infallibility, nonetheless these teachings required the attention and respect of the faithful. This is because they are given by the *Magisterium* of the Church's pastors, which succeeds from the authority of the Apostolic College to teach the Church in the name of Christ.

---

an ecumenical council. In the case of a non-defining act, a doctrine is taught infallibly by the ordinary and universal *Magisterium* of the bishops dispersed throughout the world who are in communion with the Successor of Peter. Such a doctrine can be confirmed or reaffirmed by the Roman Pontiff, even without recourse to a solemn definition, by declaring explicitly that it belongs to the teaching of the ordinary and universal *Magisterium* as a truth that is divinely revealed (first paragraph) or as a truth of Catholic doctrine (second paragraph). Consequently, when there has not been a judgment on a doctrine in the solemn form of a definition, but this doctrine, belonging to the inheritance of the *depositum fidei,* is taught by the ordinary and universal *Magisterium,* which necessarily includes the pope, such a doctrine is to be understood as having been set forth infallibly. The declaration of confirmation or reaffirmation by the Roman Pontiff in this case is not a new dogmatic definition, but a formal attestation of a truth already possessed and infallibly transmitted by the Church."

[39] For example, canon law, or decisions of the Roman congregations regarding Church practice which are offered for guidance until a particular question is studied further—1989 document *Donum Vitae* on certain procedures of assisted procreation, or historically the decisions of the Pontifical Biblical Commission on Scriptural studies which were changed over time. Cf. Dulles, *The Craft of Theology* (New York: The Crossroad Publishing Company, 1995), 111.

LEVELS OF MAGISTERIAL TEACHING AND THE RESPONSE OF THE FAITHFUL

Commentary on the 1989 *Professio Fidei* and Oath of Fidelity and the Instruction *Donum Veritatis*[40]

Given the various forms which the *Magisterium* takes in its service to both the Word of God and the Church, one can further distinguish magisterial teaching into various categories, each having a specific theological significance and each requiring a distinct degree of compliance (acceptance) by the faithful of the Church. In this, one can speak of a criteriology of sifting through the magisterial statements to assign a degree of teaching authority to the statement and the corresponding required assent. In *Lumen Gentium* no. 25, the Second Vatican Council stated generally that every doctrinal enunciation must be interpreted by considering the authority of the subject from which it came, and according to the mind and will of the subject manifest in the text which becomes clearer by considering the material treated, the nature of the document, and the tenor of the language used in the document.

Historically this was seen as one of the essential tasks of Dogmatic Theology: to assign grades of certainty to magisterial pronouncements and to determine the particular type of assent required by the faithful. In the past there were numerous grades and distinctions made by theology in this regard (often not agreed upon by all theologians).[41] However, recent magisterial teaching and instruction have simplified this task.

In the Congregation for the Doctrine of the Faith's (CDF) "Commentary on the 1989 Profession of Faith and Oath of Fidelity," and its 1990 Instructio, *Donum Veritatis*, "On the Ecclesial Vocation of the Theologian," four grades of magisterial teaching are singled out, each with a different degree of required assent. The import of these distinctions was underlined by an allocution of John Paul II to the

---

[40] See Dulles, *Magisterium,* 83-99 and Ibid., 108-111.

[41] Cf. Ludwig Ott, *Fundamentals of Catholic Dogma,* 9-10.

Plenary session of the CDF on November 29, 1995, in which the pope stated concerning the authority of the *Magisterium*:

> That this authority includes various degrees of teaching has been clearly stated in two recent documents of the CDF: the *Professio Fidei* and the Instruction *Donum Veritatis*. This hierarchy of degrees should not be considered an impediment but a stimulus to theology.[42]

Thus, it is important for a priest to be aware of these distinctions and to be able to understand their binding status.

In its Commentary on the 1989 *Professio Fidei and Oath of Fidelity* and *Donum Veritatis* nos. 13-20, 23-24, the CDF specified the various levels of magisterial teaching alluded to in the final paragraphs of the *Professio Fidei*, and made four basic distinctions in the degrees of the *Magisterium's* teaching and in the required types of assent on the part of the faithful. The four fundamental theological qualifications are as follows:

1. Definitive Declarations of Revealed Truth. In the first case are those solemn declarations concerning the content of Revelation as contained in Sacred Scripture and Tradition. These teachings are "dogmas" of the Catholic faith. Here the *Magisterium* enjoys the protection of the charism of infallibility as it declares a dogma in the strict sense of the term as a truth revealed by God to be held in faith by the entire Church. As *Donum Veritatis* states:

> Thus, it is exercised particularly when the bishops in union with their visible head proclaim a doctrine by collegial act, as is the case in an ecumenical council, or when the Roman Pontiff, fulfilling his mission as supreme Pastor and teacher of all Christians, proclaims a doctrine "ex cathedra."[43]

These definitive declarations of revealed truth can occur either by a "defining act" (solemn definition of the pope or pope and bishops in an ecumenical council) or a non-defining act (the definitive teaching of the ordinary and universal *Magisterium*). The assent required

---

[42] Cf. *L'Osservatore Romano*, November, 1995.

[43] Congregation for the Doctrine of the Faith, *Donum Veritatis*, no. 15, in Dulles, *Magisterium*.

of the Church is the adherence of theological faith, or divine and Catholic faith.

2. *Definitive Declarations of non-Revealed Truth.* The second level concerns the secondary object of the infallible *Magisterium*; i.e. those truths not *per se* contained in the deposit of faith (although in some cases, the Church at a later time after more reflection may come to a more mature perception of the deposit of revelation. In doing so the Church may determine that a particular truth previously taught as not strictly part of the deposit, in fact is and has been part of the deposit of divine revelation). Hence these truths are not directly revealed by God, but are intrinsically connected to the deposit of faith and are necessarily presupposed by the deposit of faith, without which revelation could not be guarded or properly expounded. These teachings are "truths of Catholic doctrine" and the *Magisterium* is protected by the charism of infallibility in its teaching. Here, *Donum Veritatis* states:

> ... [T]he *Magisterium* can make a pronouncement in a definitive way on propositions which, even if not contained among the truths of faith, are nonetheless intimately connected with them, in such a way, that the definitive character of such affirmations derives in the final analysis from revelation itself.[44]

These definitive declarations of non-revealed (i.e. not necessarily revealed) truth can occur either by a "defining act" (solemn definition of the pope, or pope and bishops in an ecumenical council) or a "non-defining act" (the definitive teaching of the ordinary and universal *Magisterium*). The corresponding degree of assent by the faithful is that such teaching proposed by the *Magisterium* to be held in a definitive way must be "firmly held and accepted," i.e. given definitive assent (*assensus definitivum*).

3. *Non-Definitive Obligatory Teaching.* The third level of teaching and the corresponding assent regards the successors of the Apostles teaching in communion with the successor of Peter. In a particular way, it regards the Roman Pontiff as Pastor of the entire Church in the exercise of the ordinary universal *Magisterium* of the Church when this does not issue an infallible definition or a definitive

---

[44] Ibid., no. 16.

pronouncement. Rather, it is in the proposal of some teaching which leads to a better understanding of revelation in matters of faith and morals.

Divine assistance is seen to be provided the *Magisterium* in its role by the Holy Spirit, and this divine assistance provides the motive for the assent required by the faithful of the Church. Here, *Donum Veritatis* is clear: "The willingness to submit loyally to the teaching of the *Magisterium* on matters *per se* not irreformable must be the rule."[45] Here the assent required is that of religious submission of intellect and will (*obsequium religiousum*). In this regard, the Instruction states: "This kind of response cannot be simply exterior or disciplinary but must be understood within the logic of faith and under the impulse of the obedience to the faith."[46] To this level of magisterial teaching belong the day-to-day teaching of the pope and bishops regarding matters of faith or morals that are not necessarily proposed in a definitive way. Given the guidance of the Holy Spirit, one must presume until otherwise informed that this teaching is true and not erroneous. The benefit of doubt lies with the *Magisterium*.

4. Prudential Judgments. The fourth level of magisterial teaching and the corresponding assent regards interventions of the *Magisterium* in the prudential order; thus, it involves prudential judgments of the *Magisterium* in debated questions or even matters of discipline in Church life. Here the *Magisterium* exercises its mission to serve the people of God by warning them of dangerous opinions which could lead to error. The mission is also exercised by issuing laws and rules of conduct and procedure. In this the *Magisterium* employs not only solidly established principles of faith but also certain contingent or conjectural elements; hence, prudential judgments.[47]

In this it often only becomes possible after the passing of time to discern what is necessary in the judgment and what is contingent. Here the *Magisterium* in its documents may not be free of deficiencies, for the bishops and their advisors may not have always considered

---

[45] Ibid., no. 24.

[46] Ibid., no. 23.

[47] For example, the second part of *Gaudium et Spes*, judgments of the Roman Congregations regarding certain disputed matters, in the past questions of the interpretation of Sacred Scripture or in the present questions concerning the moral legitimacy of certain forms of artificial procreation.

every aspect or the entire complexity of the question at hand.[48] What is required of the faithful is the willingness to give the assent of loyal submission to the *Magisterium* as guided in its mission by the Holy Spirit. While at times these prudential judgments may be reconsidered or reversed after further consideration of the question at hand, nonetheless, as *Donum Veritatis* no. 24 states:

> But it would be contrary to the truth, if, proceeding from some particular cases, one were to conclude that the Church's *Magisterium* can be habitually mistaken in its prudential judgments, or that it does not enjoy divine assistance in the integral exercise of its mission ... The willingness to submit loyally to the *Magisterium* on matters *per se* not irreformable must be the rule.[49]

CONCLUSION

One of the central aspects of the ministry and mission of priests is that of proclaiming the Gospel through teaching and explaining the deposit of the Church's faith. In this reflection we examined the role or ministry of the priest as teacher. We saw that while priests do not directly exercise a *Magisterium* in the sense of the bishops who teach the Church in the name of Christ, they do represent the *Magisterium* of the pope and bishops in the teaching of the faithful entrusted to their care. So, they must present to the faithful the official magisterial teaching of the Church. In treating the mission of priests as "heralds and transmitters of the faith," the *Directory on the Ministry and Life of Priests* states: "Such ministry, developed within the hierarchical community, enables him to authoritatively express the Catholic faith and give *official* testimony of the faith of the Church."[50]

This means that rather than presenting their own ideas and theories or those of theologians, priests must endeavor to preach and teach as the faith and doctrine of the Church only that which has

---

[48] Congregation for the Doctrine of the Faith, *Donum Veritatis*, no. 24 in Dulles, *Magisterium*.

[49] Ibid.

[50] Congregation for the Clergy, *Directory on the Ministry and Life of Priests*, no. 45.

been put forward by the teaching office of the Church: the *Magisterium* of the pope and bishops, as the faith and doctrine of the Catholic Church. Priests teach primarily by preaching and catechesis, and this directly "concerns proclaiming a Word that cannot be altered, because it has been entrusted to the Church in order to protect, penetrate and faithfully transmit."[51]

The authoritative interpreter of the Word of God is the *Magisterium* of the pope and bishops. So for priests to be faithful and effective pastoral teachers of the Catholic faith, it is important that they know and understand the various ways the Church's *Magisterium* is exercised, the various forms it takes, and the levels of teaching that it issues. In this way they will be truly men of the Church, transmitting the Gospel in its fullness for the salvation of all.

REFLECTION QUESTIONS

1. How seriously do I take my role as a teacher of the faith through my exercise of preaching and catechesis? Do I take an adequate amount of time preparing my homily by prayer, study and reflection? Am I involved in catechetical instruction and what do I do to prepare for this?

2. Do I realize my role as a representative of the *Magisterium* of the Church? Have I developed a sensitivity and docility to the living Tradition of the Church and her *Magisterium*? Do I strive to embody in myself an *anima ecclesiastica* always thinking with the mind and intention of the Church?

3. Do I read attentively and study the documents and teaching of the *Magisterium*? Am I able to present these teachings and explain them to the faithful to whom I have been entrusted? Am I familiar with the *Catechism of the Catholic Church* and can I direct the faithful to further resources when they have questions and need more direction?

4. Do I understand the various levels of magisterial teaching and the response of obedience required by the faithful to these levels? Do I have issues with the teaching of the *Magisterium,* and do

---

[51] Ibid.

these issues hinder me from presenting the authentic teaching of the Church to the faithful in my homilies and catechetical instruction? Do I always strive to preach and teach as the faith and doctrine of the Church that which the *Magisterium* of the Church has put forward as the faith and doctrine of the Catholic Church? Or do I present my own ideas and theories, or those of others? Do I strive in my ministry as a priest representing Jesus the Teacher to be a faithful and effective pastoral teacher of the Catholic faith, to transmit the Gospel in its fullness for the salvation of all?

SUGGESTED READINGS

Congregation for the Clergy. *Directory on the Ministry and Life of Priests.* Vatican City: Libera Editrice Vaticana, 1994.

Dictionary of Fundamental Theology, edited by R. Latourelle and R. Fisichella. New York: The Crossroad Publishing Company, 1994.

Dulles, Avery. *Magisterium.* Naples, FL: Sapientia Press, 2007. See Appendices.

_____. The Craft of Theology. 2nd ed. New York: Crossroad Publications, 1995.

Galot, Jean. *Theology of the Priesthood.* San Francisco: Ignatius Press, 1985.

Latourelle, René. *Theology of Revelation.* New York: Alba House, 1987.

Miller, Frederick L. *The Grace of Ars.* San Francisco: Ignatius Press, 2010. See Appendices.

Nichols, Aidan. *The Shape of Catholic Theology.* Edinburgh: T&T Clark, 1991.

O'Connor, James T. *The Gift of Infallibility.* San Francisco: Ignatius Press, 2008.

Pope John Paul II. *Holy Thursday Letters to My Brother Priests.* Chicago: Midwest Theological Forum, 1992.

Ratzinger, Joseph. Letter July 9, 2004. "Worthiness to Receive Holy Communion: General Principles". See http://www.catholicculture.org/culture/library/ view. cfm?recnum=6041 (accessed May 7, 2010).

Wicks, Jared. *Doing Theology.* Mahwah: Paulist Press, 2009.

Chapter Four

MEN OF COMPASSION:
PRIESTS AND FORGIVENESS

Rev. Dennis J. Billy, C.Ss.R.

Did you ever hear the story of how Jesus one day made a clandestine visit to earth? He came upon a crippled man sitting along the roadside, took pity on him, and straightened his legs. A little further along, He came upon a blind man, had mercy on him, and gave him back his sight. Still further on, He came upon a deaf man, was moved with compassion, and opened his ears. Finally, He came upon a Catholic priest sitting on the curb, crying his heart out. Jesus asked him what was wrong, and the priest sobbed uncontrollably, "I was just made a pastor—and the parish is millions of dollars in debt!" At that, Jesus sat down beside the troubled priest, placed a hand on his shoulder, cast His eyes to the ground—and He too began to weep![1] I'm not going to tell you if those were tears of joy or sadness. Let me just say that compassion means "suffering with someone," and Jesus was (and is) particularly good at it.

FROM JERUSALEM TO JERICHO

When I hear the word *compassion,* I often think of another unfortunate traveler in dire need of roadside assistance, the man who fell prey to robbers in Jesus' parable of the Good Samaritan (Lk 10:25-37). We all know the story and it hardly bears repeating. While on the road from Jerusalem to Jericho, a man is ambushed, stripped, beaten,

---

[1] Adapted from the Internet site "my-pastor.com," accessed January 31, 2010, http://www.my-pastor.com/pastor-jokes.html.

robbed, and left on the side of the road to die. Two of his own Jewish countrymen see him, yet pass him by without lifting a finger to help. It is only a stranger, a foreigner, a lowly Samaritan, who takes pity on him and comes to his aid.

For our purposes this evening, what strikes me most about the parable is that Jesus identifies a priest and a Levite, two members of the priestly tribe of Levi, as those lacking in compassion. It may very well be that these men actually thought they were serving God by avoiding the dying man, out of a fear of becoming unclean and hence unfit to perform their ritual temple duties in Jerusalem. Such a reason, however, does not excuse them and actually makes the lesson of Jesus' parable all the more powerful. Compassion, He is telling us, is a fundamental quality of Christian discipleship. In His kingdom, everyone is our neighbor. In His kingdom, compassion is the law of the land. In His kingdom, priests must be compassionate and forgiving before all else. If they are not, they simply are not following the way of the Lord Jesus.

Today's priests wear many hats. They are preachers, teachers, administrators, community leaders, confessors, spiritual directors, celebrants—to name but a few of the many roles they play in the life of the Church. In performing their duties, they must always remember that, by virtue of their ordination, they are closely conformed to the person of Christ and thus called upon to possess the same attitudes that He displayed in His life and ministry. Simply put: priests are called to think, speak, and act in conformity with the example of Jesus.[2] If they do not, then there is a gap between the kind of priests they are and the kind of priests Jesus is calling them to be.

The question before us is whether, over time, the gap is getting larger or smaller. Most priests I meet would admit that, to some extent, such a gap *does* exist in their lives and would explain it in terms of human weakness and their own personal sinfulness. Most would also admit that they sincerely desire to bring the compassionate love of Christ to those they serve. After all, why else were they ordained? In our suspicious, quick-to-judge, scandal-laden world, it certainly is not for the honor and status once afforded them. Nor is

---

[2] Acting in conformity with the example of Jesus is one of the fundamental Biblical criteria for moral reflection. Cf. Pontifical Biblical Commission, *The Bible and Morality: Biblical Roots of Christian Conduct*, nos. 100-102 (Vatican City: Libreria Editrice Vaticana, 2008), 137-141.

it for the hours they work or the accommodations given them. And it is certainly not for the pay! So what motivates them?

Saint John Vianney, the Curé of Ars, whose 150th anniversary of death we are celebrating during this Year for Priests, once described the priesthood as "the love of the heart of Jesus." "When you see a priest," he wrote, "think of Our Lord Jesus Christ."[3] The reason a man is ordained a priest, the saint of Ars is telling us, is simply to bring Christ's love to others. To do so, they must be men of heart, men of forgiveness, and men of compassion.

CHRIST'S COMPASSION, CHRIST'S PASSION

In Christian spirituality, the word "compassion" has many nuances and is difficult to pin down. Although it is often identified with such terms as "mercy," "pity," and "tenderness," its distinct meaning is to express "the empathetic attachment of one being to another."[4] It has been described as "the capacity to be attracted and moved by the fragility, weakness, and suffering of another."[5] Compassion, which comes from the Latin *compassio*, meaning "to suffer with," is "the ability to be vulnerable enough to undergo risk and loss for the good of the other."[6] It is not merely helping another person or group of people, but identifying with their experience on such a profound level of one's being that one is moved to alleviate their pain and even share in their suffering.

I am reminded of Elie Wiesel's description of a young boy who was hanged in the Buchenwald concentration camp during the Second World War before his fellow prisoners, all of whom were forced to walk by and observe him at close range. Once the chair was kicked from under his legs, it took more than half an hour for him to die. As the boy was choking at the neck and writhing in pain during

---

[3] Cited in Abbé Francis Trochu, *The Curé of Ars: A Biography of St. Jean-Marie Vianney*, trans. Ronald Matthews (Manila: Sinag-Tala Publishers, 1986), 103. Cf. also *Catechism of the Catholic Church*, no. 1589.

[4] *The New Dictionary of Catholic Spirituality* (Collegeville, MN: The Liturgical Press, 1993), s.v. "Compassion," by Michael Downey.

[5] Ibid.

[6] Ibid.

a slow, torturous death, someone whispered while standing in line, "Where is the merciful God, where is He? ... For God's sake, where is God?" Wiesel's response captures the meaning of compassion: "And from within me, I heard a voice answer: Where is He? This is where—hanging from this gallows ... "[7] The boy's suffering, in Wiesel's experience, had become God's: the two were intimately one.

For Christians, Jesus represents the fullness of compassion. As Emmanuel, "God is with us" (Mt 1:23), He reveals to us through His life and ministry the compassion of God, whom He called "Abba, Father!" (Rom 8:15). The Gospels are full of examples of His compassionate love for humanity: "In the New Testament, Jesus exemplifies God's compassion in his preaching and healing (Mt 9:6; 14:4), in his concern for lost humanity (Lk 19:41), and in his sacrificial love on the cross (Rom 5:8)."[8] What is more, the Scriptures tell us that "[t]he followers of Jesus are to live lives of compassion as an expression of the love that Jesus enjoined (Mt 5:4-7; Jn 13:34; Jas 2:8-18; 1 Jn 3:18)."[9] In the Gospels, moreover, "Jesus provided paradigms of compassion in the parables of the good Samaritan, who had compassion on the wounded traveler (Lk 10:33), and the prodigal son, whose father saw him in the distance and, 'moved with compassion,' ran to meet him (Lk 15:20)."[10]

Jesus' compassion stemmed from His relationship with His Father in heaven. He wanted that relationship to be the paradigm for all human relationships. In a world overwhelmed by sin and suffering, however, He understood that the only way to achieve this end would be not merely to empathize with the suffering of others, but to embrace it as His own. He knew that an authentic and true compassion for humanity would ultimately lead to His own passion and death. Compassion, in other words, ultimately manifests itself in passion.

One author who sees the intrinsic link between Jesus' compassion and passion is the Jesuit theologian, John Navone. In his book,

---

[7] Elie Wiesel, *Night*, trans. Marion Wiesel (New York: Hill and Wang, 2006), 64-65.

[8] *The New Dictionary of Catholic Spirituality*, s.v. "Compassion," by Michael Downey.

[9] Ibid.

[10] Ibid.

Gospel Love: A Narrative Theology, he outlines "the link between the compassion of Jesus and his passion."[11] He writes:

> The compassion of Jesus or his "suffering with" reaches its culmination in his passion, his "suffering for." In his compassion he moved to his passion, which John portrays as his loving "unto the end" (13:1). The compassion of Jesus becomes his passion as the final and ultimate sign of his being-in-Love. The passion is the culmination, or final moment, of his compassion. The sign of the kingdom's coming is realized when compassion with others leads to passion for others: "A man can have no greater love than to lay down his life for his friends" (Jn 15:13). Compassion must become passion for the disciple as well as for the master, for this is the ultimate measure of our being-in-Love, in the Spirit that is the life of mutual indwelling of Father and Son.[12]

By entering into the fullness of human suffering, by not only "suffering *with* us," but by also "suffering *for* us," Jesus established a new bond between humanity and divinity. Jesus, the God-man, who suffered and died for humanity, gathered all of humanity into Himself and paid the awful price for humanity's tragic flaw, the primordial desire to become God without God, to be Creator rather than creature, to make ourselves the center of the universe rather than the One from whom our origin stems. Jesus' passion and death, the ultimate expression of God's compassion for humanity, overcame the sin of human origins and put us back in right relationship with the Father as His adopted sons and daughters.

Jesus' solidarity with humanity, His desire "to suffer with" and "for us" was an integral part of His priestly dignity. He sacrificed Himself on our behalf; that is, He made us holy (*sacrum facere*), so we might enjoy life with Him in the presence of the Father. Even now, He intercedes for us and mediates the grace of the Holy Spirit to us all because of the love He shares with the Father. The compassion of the Father manifests itself in the priestly compassion and passion of

---

[11] John Navone, *Gospel Love: A Narrative Theology* (Wilmington, DE: Michael Glazier, 1984), 107.

[12] Ibid., 107-108.

Christ. The same holds true for all who share in His priestly life and ministry.

A wonderful example of a priest who not only "suffered with," but also "suffered for" others was Maximilian Kolbe, a Conventual Franciscan who, as a prisoner of war at Auschwitz volunteered to die for one of his inmates with these words: "I am a Polish Catholic priest," he said. "I am old. I want to take this man's place because he has a wife and children." After saying these words, Kolbe was taken out of the line, led into a starvation block, and left there to die a slow, painful death.[13] Here was someone whose compassion for another led him to make the ultimate sacrifice.

FROM PASSION TO FORGIVENESS

Jesus' compassion reached its fullness in His passion, one of the major effects of which was His intercessory prayer from the Cross, "Father, forgive them, they know not what they do" (Lk 23:34). Early on in His public ministry, He called the merciful blessed and assured them that they would receive mercy (Mt 5:7). He told His followers to be compassionate as their Father in heaven was compassionate (Lk 6:36). He taught them to offer no resistance, to turn the other cheek, to love their enemies and pray for their persecutors (Mt 5: 39, 44). His words from the Cross demonstrate that He lived what He taught—even in death. Compassion, in His mind, was the path to happiness, the way to true beatitude.

For most of us, forgiving someone who hurt us is very difficult. It usually involves a long, drawn-out process of claiming the hurt; overcoming guilt for whatever role we might have played in causing it; finally recognizing that we were victimized; reacting to it in righteous anger; and then, moving to wholeness and mutual acceptance.[14] When asked how many times we should forgive our neighbors, Jesus responded not seven times, but seventy times seven times (Mt 18:22). This startling response demonstrates how central the act of forgiveness was to Jesus' life and mission.

---

[13] Bert Ghezzi, *Voices of the Saints: A Year of Readings* (New York: Doubleday, 2000), 520.

[14] Cf. William A. Meninger, *The Process of Forgiveness* (New York: Continuum, 1997), 48-72.

Although not easy to achieve, forgiving actually becomes less difficult over time. Believe it or not, the more we forgive those who hurt us, the less effort it requires. If we make it a priority in our lives, we gradually find that a deeply rooted attitude has grown within us, one that enables us to face life and all that happens to us with a gentle, forgiving heart. Such an attitude comes not through human effort alone, but in conjunction with God's grace. True forgiveness, you see, is a sign of God's presence in our midst. It is a gift from the Lord, one for which all of us should be deeply grateful.

Jesus possessed such a gentle, forgiving heart. His entire life was about healing and forgiving. It came easy for Him because He did it so often and because of His deep, intimate union with the Father. When He asks His Father to forgive His tormentors, He does so from a heart that, within a short while, would be pierced by the lance of one of the very men He is forgiving. By asking His Father to forgive, He teaches us that to hurt another person deliberately and unjustly is also a sin against God Himself. As a result, the person who hurts another in this way ultimately hurts himself or herself in the process.

This self-inflicted wound is what Jesus sees when He looks down from the Cross and gazes upon His tormentors. Moved with compassion for them, He turns to His Father in heaven and intercedes on their behalf. He does the same for us whenever we injure ourselves in this way. Through His death, He takes our sins upon Himself and pleads our cause. He is also asking His Father in heaven to forgive all of humanity. For this reason, His death on the Cross is a key moment in the history of salvation. It is a primary means by which death lost its stranglehold over the human race. As one might expect, it has special significance for priests.

PRIESTLY COMPASSION, PRIESTLY PASSION, PRIESTLY FORGIVENESS

The priest is *alter Christus* ("another Christ"). At his ordination, he is conformed to Christ in the very depths of his being. Because of the priestly character that marks his soul, he participates in Christ's ministry and life in a unique way, one that empowers him to administer the sacraments and to bring the presence of Christ to others in a concrete and visible way. For this reason, all that has been said of

Christ's passion, compassion, and forgiveness, applies to him in a special way. Because he is a priest, he acts *in persona Christi* ("in the person of Christ").

Saint John Vianney was someone very conscious of the great dignity of the priesthood and who manifested these important qualities of Christ's priesthood in his life and ministry. Conformed unto Christ by virtue of his priestly ordination, he focused all his energies to live his vocation to the fullest and to be and act in the person of Christ in everything he did and with everyone he met. This close bond with the Lord's high priesthood, nurtured by a deep thirst for holiness, an intense prayer life, and heightened desire to serve God's people, enabled him to think, speak, and act in conformity with the example of Jesus. Because of this close bond with the Lord, he was able to "suffer *with* his people" (compassion), "suffer *for* his people" (passion), and extend God's merciful love *to* them through his priestly ministry, especially in the confessional (forgiveness).

Every dimension of Saint John Vianney's priestly life and ministry can be understood in terms of his compassionate desire to help others "experience the Lord's merciful love:"[15] His ministry of preaching, his catechetical instructions, his anointing of the sick, his visiting the poor and homebound, his work in *La Providence* (the small orphanage he founded), his time in the confessional for reconciliation and the direction of souls (often eleven or twelve and, in the warmer months, as many as eighteen hours a day), his celebration of the Holy Sacrifice of the Mass.[16] He saw all of his life and ministry as an expression of the compassionate love of God made manifest in the person of Jesus Christ, on whose behalf he was ministering to the people of Ars. He was deeply aware that Christ was living a mystical life through the members of his body, the Church, and that, as an ordained priest, he had a special mission to teach, govern, and sanctify the people entrusted to his care.

It is no small sign of esteem and deep regard that, in his letter proclaiming a Year for Priests, Pope Benedict XVI wrote: "In his time the Curé of Ars was able to transform the hearts and the lives of so many people because he enabled them to experience the Lord's

---

[15] See below n. 17.

[16] Cf. Trochu, *The Curé of Ars*, 49-58, 68-75, 94-114.

merciful love. Our own time urgently needs a similar proclamation and witness to the truth of Love: *Deus caritas est* (1 Jn 4:8)."[17]

All priests have this same task before them in their life and ministry. "Whatever the priest may be," the Curé of Ars liked to say, "he is still the instrument that the good God makes use of to distribute his holy Word. You pour liquor through a funnel; whether it be made of gold or copper, if the liquor is good it will still be good."[18] The Curé's life reminds us that, in addition to the compassion of Christ manifested to others through their preaching and sacramental ministry, all priests are also called to live the life of the Beatitudes. This is so others will see Christ and experience His merciful love through their holiness of life. He reminds us that all priests should strive to become holy priests so Christ's merciful love will shine through their lives all the more clearly. Holy priests are, first and foremost, men of compassion: they "suffer with" their people; they "suffer for" their people; they forgive their people, because they themselves have experienced the wonder and grace of God's merciful love. As the Pontifical Biblical Commission reminds us in *The Bible and Morality: Biblical Roots of Christian Conduct*,

> [d]isciples who strive to imitate Jesus are told to adopt a way of life that reflects now the future reality of the kingdom; they must show compassion, not respond to violence, avoid sexual exploitation, take the initiative in reconciliation and love their enemies. Such dispositions ... characterize the new life in the kingdom of God. Of these, reconciliation, pardon and unconditional love are central.[19]

Saint John Vianney was one such disciple. As one biographer notes, "It was his love of God and his enthusiasm for the glory of

---

[17] Pope Benedict XVI, "Letter Proclaiming a Year of Priests on the 150th Anniversary of the *Dies Natalis* of the Curé of Ars," June 16, 2009 (Philadelphia, PA: Office for Worship, 2009), 4, accessed February 2, 2010, http://www.vatican.va/holy_father/benedict_xvi/letters/2009/documents/ hf_ben-xvi_let_20090616_anno-sacerdotale_en.html.

[18] Cited in *Magnificat, Year for Priests Companion* (2009), 12.

[19] Pontifical Biblical Commission, *The Bible and Morality*, no. 102, p. 141.

God that inspired in the Curé of Ars such an immeasurable devotion for souls and such a compassion for sinners."[20]

TOWARDS A SPIRITUALITY OF PRIESTLY COMPASSION

But just what does this mean in the concrete activities of a priest's daily life? What practical suggestions can we make for those priests who desperately seek to narrow the gap, who recognize the importance of living for Christ, yet who recognize in their own lives the vast distance between the ideal and the real, between the kind of priests they desire to be and the kind of priests they really are? How do they narrow the gap, especially when they tried and tried so much in their spiritual lives and, in the end, feel, for whatever reasons, that they fell short?

There are no easy answers to such difficult and probing questions. If spirituality, as Ronald Rolheiser suggests, is "what we do with the fire within us,"[21] then all we can do is try to identify that fire and offer some concrete suggestions for how priests ministering in today's Church can harness it in a constructive and truly compassionate way. *Pastores Dabo Vobis*, Pope John Paul II's Post-Synodal Apostolic Exhortation on the priesthood, is a good place to begin, for it reminds us that "for every priest his spiritual formation is the core which unifies and gives life to his *being* a priest and his *acting as* a priest."[22] Everything a priest does, in other words, should flow from his relationship with Christ. Only by being on fire with the love of Christ can he hope to pass that love on to others. For this to happen, however, priests need specific spiritual guidelines ("rules of thumb," if you will) to help them get in touch with their deep passion for God so they may foster a spirituality of compassion in their lives and ministries that will lessen the gap in their experience between

---

[20] Trochu, *The Curé of Ars*, 151-152.

[21] Ronald Rolheiser, *The Holy Longing: The Search for A Christian Spirituality* (New York: Doubleday, 1999), 11.

[22] Pope John Paul II, *Pastores Dabo Vobis*, no. 45; cf. also United States Conference of Catholic Bishops, *Program of Priestly Formation*, 5th ed., no. 115.

the ideal and the real with each new day. The five that follow are not exhaustive and are merely intended to point in the right direction.

To begin with, priests must humbly acknowledge their short-comings by means of a daily review of life, regular sacramental Confession, and ongoing spiritual direction. It is important for priests to acknowledge where they are in their relationship with the Lord and where they would like to be. The Gospels remind us again and again that Jesus' earliest followers were weak, vulnerable men, who were full of imperfections and human foibles, some of which were quite visible, like Peter's brashness and Thomas's doubting, and others which were hidden in the dark, shadowy places within them and would come out only in moments of crisis and deep peril. After all, they all ran away and left Him to face His enemies all alone (Mt 26:56). In one way or another, they all denied Him and on some level, even betrayed Him; it is important for us to remember that priests, too, have done the same at various moments in their lives. Priests are ordained to serve. It is important for them to remember that there are times in their own lives when they, too, may simply want to wash their hands of everything and walk away. The Apostles did it. Saint John Vianney entertained the idea and, at times, even attempted it.[23] The same can also be said of most priests.

The question before them is: how will they react to their human shortcomings? Will they deny them, bury them deep inside, project them onto others, or numb the pain they cause by anesthetizing themselves with drugs or alcohol? If they are not careful, the burdens of their weaknesses, human shortcomings, and sins will take their toll. To be men of compassion and men of forgiveness, they first of all need to take a good hard look at themselves and acknowledge where they are in their relationship with the Lord. They need to admit their faults to themselves, to those they have hurt, and especially to God. The ministers of the sacrament of Reconciliation must also be ministered by it. Those who give direction from the pulpit, in the confessional, and in the parlor, must also be willing to receive it. To put it simply, to be men of compassion, priests must humbly acknowledge how they themselves have fallen short, and then use the well-tried spiritual means available to them to discern where the Lord is leading them in their lives. Pope John Paul II puts it so well in

---

[23] Trochu, *The Curé of Ars*, 117-120.

Reconciliatio et Paenitentia, his Post-Synodal Apostolic Exhortation on the sacrament of Penance:

> The priest's celebration of the Eucharist and administration of the other Sacraments, his pastoral zeal, his relationship with the faithful, his communion with his brother priests, his collaboration with his Bishop, his life of prayer—in a word, the whole of his priestly existence, suffers an inexorable decline if by negligence or for some other reason he fails to receive the Sacrament of Penance at regular intervals and in a spirit of genuine faith and devotion. If a priest were no longer to go to confession or properly confess his sins, his *priestly being* and his *priestly action* would feel its effects very soon, and this would also be noticed by the community of which he was the pastor.[24]

The bottom line for priests? Examine your conscience daily. Go to Confession regularly. Seek out a wise and holy spiritual director.

Priests must foster their relationship with God through intimate and heartfelt prayer. In addition to acknowledging their faults and failings, priests must recognize their need for God's help to overcome them. They need to humble themselves before the Lord, open their hearts to Him, and place all of their worries, concerns, sins, moral imperfections, and spiritual wants in his hands. They need to take responsibility for their actions and seek forgiveness not only for their actions, but also for the deeply rooted attitudes of self-centeredness that lie behind so many of them. Sharing with the Lord from the heart, meditation or what is sometimes referred to as "mental prayer," is a fundamental prerequisite for anyone wishing to have an intimate relationship with Him.

Spiritual writers tell us that intimacy results from a combination of self-disclosure and loving attention.[25] If this is so, then to be intimate with the Lord means that priests are willing to share everything about themselves with Him, as one friend to another, and also to

---

[24] Pope John Paul II, *Reconciliatio et Paenitentia*, no. 31.

[25] See, for example, Pat Collins, *Intimacy and the Hungers of the Heart* (Dublin/Mystic, CT: The Columba Press/Twenty-Third Publications, 1991), 142.

spend time with Him in prayer, and especially before His presence in the Blessed Sacrament.

Priests cannot be true men of compassion if they do not have an intimate friendship with Christ. As priests, they cannot announce "the love of the heart of Jesus" if they are not deeply touched by a personal knowledge of that love. They cannot dispense forgiveness to others if they themselves never experienced it. It was Jesus' intimate relationship with the Father which led Him to suffer *with* others, suffer *for* others, and ask forgiveness for the sins of humanity while hanging from the Cross. It is certainly true that those who minister in Christ's name do so because they are ontologically configured to Him at ordination. It is also true that when they administer the sacraments, Christ works through them regardless of their personal failings and lack of holiness. At the same time, as Saint John Vianney, priests should also be deeply aware of the transforming power of grace and its power to illumine their minds, strengthen their wills, and free their passions from their base, sinful tendencies so they might give their hearts totally to God and be passionately in love with Him.

Jesus wants His priests to be good priests, holy priests, compassionate priests, and forgiving priests. He wants them to be redeemed; fully alive. He wants them to be saints. The bottom line for priests? Make a daily holy hour. Break it up into smaller parts, if necessary. You won't regret it. It will do you much good. In time, you'll even come to enjoy it and look forward to the time you spend with the Lord.

Priests must cultivate intimate friendships and supports that will allow them to share burdens with others and receive honest feedback about the appropriateness of their actions and decisions. Besides acknowledging their failings and turning to God for help, priests must not be afraid to allow their weaknesses and vulnerability to show. The Apostle Paul once wrote that it was when he was weak that he was strong (2 Cor 12:10). By this he meant that he was not relying on his own strength, but on the power of God working through his human weakness.

The power of the Gospel shines through those who acknowledge their faults and trust in the Lord's saving grace. Being human, priests can easily be masters of self-deception, convincing themselves, perhaps not in their minds, but possibly in their hearts, that they are building the kingdom primarily through their own efforts, and that Jesus is only a secondary figure in the ordinary day-to-day affairs of Church life. If they manage to convince themselves of this, they will often try to hide their weaknesses—wear a disguise, if you will—so they come off as the master preacher, teacher, confessor, administrator, or what have you. Priests need to allow God to be God in their lives and, in doing so, allow themselves to be themselves, and also allow the people they serve to see them for who they truly are. They need to be authentic, genuine, and sincere. They need to be humble. "Humility is to walk in truth," we are told.[26]

People can always spot a fake, someone who, like the Pharisees criticized by Jesus in the Gospels, were more concerned with external appearances than the purity of their hearts. I am not saying that priests need to wear their emotions on their sleeves, or that they should not make the appropriate distinctions between the internal and external forums, or that they should try to speak to everyone as if they were speaking to their spiritual directors. What I am saying is that priests need to be comfortable in their own skins and they should not be afraid to be with the people they serve and share the Gospel with them from their hearts. They should be able to witness to the people they serve of how the power of the Gospel has touched their own lives. They need to be what the late Henri J. M. Nouwen called "wounded healers."[27]

By inviting their people into their own lives in this way, the people will be more and more willing to allow them to enter their own. Only then will priests be able to suffer with them. Only then will they be able to be men of compassion and forgiveness. The bottom line for priests? Cultivate a close circle of friends who will both support and challenge you in your priesthood. Let some of your brother priests be numbered among them. Let them get to know you. They will keep you honest with yourself and help you to be honest with God and others.

---

[26] Teresa of Avila, *Interior Castle*, 6.10, trans. E. Allison Peers, Commentary by Dennis Billy (Notre Dame, IN: Christian Classics, 2007), 248.

[27] Cf. Henri J.M. Nouwen, *The Wounded Healer: Ministry in Contemporary Society* (Garden City, NY: Doubleday, 1972).

Priests need to cultivate the contemplative capacity to recognize the invisible presence of Christ in their midst in everything they do. As bearers of Christ to others, priests must live in deep personal communion and friendship with Him and be so closely identified with Him that the narrative of His life and ministry and of His passion, death and resurrection becomes their own. When they encounter others, they carry this deep personal friendship with Christ with them, and they use the narrative of Christ's paschal mystery as the interpretative filter through which they make sense out of all that happens to them and to the people they serve.

As a result, they should mediate the presence of Christ to the people they serve and be a constant reminder to them that love, not chaos, lies at the root of all existence. Because they are men of faith and because of their close personal union with Christ, they also call the people they serve to delve beneath the level of appearances in order to deepen their faith and encounter the person of Christ in their own lives. As priests, Christ acts through them whenever they administer the sacraments. As friends of Christ, they carry His Spirit within their hearts wherever they go and have the opportunity to share that Spirit with everyone they meet. Priests are called "to live the Gospel on a deep level of consciousness" so the people they serve might do the same.[28]

Holy priests see an intimate relationship between their lives and their ministries. They see themselves as disciples of Christ and wish to follow Him not on a part-time basis, or whenever it is convenient for them, or whenever they are "on duty" (so to speak), but at every moment of their lives. They understand that they are priests *forever* and that *forever* begins in the *here and now*. If Christ reigns in a priest's heart, if the desire to follow Him is foremost, if he allows the Spirit to express itself through his own weaknesses and vulnerabilities, it will then be easy for him to be someone who reaches out and is able not only to suffer with, but also suffer for others. He will find it easier to forgive himself for his own failings before God, to seek forgiveness for his sins, to forgive those who hurt him, and to extend that forgiveness to others. The bottom line for priests? Slow down.

---

[28] For the phrase "living the Gospel at a deep level of consciousness," see William Johnston, *Mystical Theology: The Science of Love* (London: HarperCollins, 1995), 9.

Look around at what's happening in your ministry and in your life. Foster in yourself a contemplative attitude toward life. Try to live in the present moment and savor its texture, depth, and richness.

Finally, priests must become experts in the art of forgiveness. They understand that forgiveness was proclaimed by Jesus as a sign of God's presence in their midst. They know that Jesus died on the Cross and gave us the New Covenant of His Body and Blood, "so that sins may be forgiven."[29] What is more, whenever they pronounce the words of absolution upon a repentant sinner, they understand that the Lord is working through them in a powerful way. Just as Jesus forgave the sins of the paralytic (Lk 5:17-26), He now forgives all who come to them paralyzed by sinful habits and who committed actions harmful to others and to their own souls.

Priests understand that forgiveness involves a deep personal encounter with the Lord and that the Lord chose them to stand in a privileged place to see the deep spiritual wounds of those they serve and to reach out to them with words of healing and consolation. Whenever they hear confessions, they remember that they, too, are sinners and they too must seek forgiveness for their own sins. They see themselves as those who both heal and receive healing. They are humbled by the enormous trust the faithful place in them, and they do their best to step out of the way so that the Lord can work through them "to bring glad tidings to the poor. . . .to proclaim liberty to captives and recovery of sight to the blind, to let the oppressed go free and to proclaim a year acceptable to the Lord" (Lk 4:18-19).[30]

Forgiveness, for the priest, is "the love of the heart of Jesus" made manifest in the lives of the faithful in a concrete way. Priests proclaim forgiveness, because they are men of compassion, because they are followers of the way, because they are rooted in the love of the heart of Christ. They "suffer with" those who reveal their sins to them as they extend the healing hands of Christ and utter the healing words of absolution. As ministers of the sacrament of Reconciliation, they witness the healing of souls and the renewal of relationships with God,

---

[29] *The Sacramentary: The Roman Missal Revised by Decree of the Second Vatican Ecumenical Council and Published By Authority of Pope Paul VI* (New York: Catholic Book Publishing Co., 1985), 548.

[30] Cf. also Is 61:1.

with others, and with the self. They do so by being compassionate to those who come to them, yet also by being servants of the truth.[31]

When in the confessional or reconciliation room, priests remember how Jesus acted toward those who came to Him: "Has no one condemned you?" (Jn 8:10). "[Y]our sins are forgiven" (Lk 5:20). "Go, and from now on do not sin any more" (Jn 8:11). The bottom line for priests? Be the spiritual father God wants you to be. Try to forgive those who hurt you. If you cannot, ask God for help. Be gentle yet firm with those who come to you for Confession. Be first a father, then a doctor, then a teacher, and lastly a judge.[32] Be gentle yet firm also with yourself.

CONCLUSION

At the end of my reflection on priestly compassion, I would like to return to Jesus' parable of the Good Samaritan and, in particular, to a spiritual interpretation of it from the Church fathers. In contrast to the priest and Levite, who as we saw in my opening remarks are the examples par excellence of men lacking in compassion, authors such as Irenaeus of Lyons, Clement of Alexandria, Origen, Ambrose, Augustine, and John Chrysostom associate the Good Samaritan with Christ; the dying man, with fallen humanity; the oil, wine, and dressing of the dying man's wounds, with the sacraments; the inn, with the Church; the innkeeper, with the Apostles and their successors; and the eventual return of the Good Samaritan, with Christ's second coming.[33]

The parable, according to this interpretation, reminds us that humanity's healing was made possible by Christ's compassionate

---

[31] Cf. Pope John Paul II, *Reconciliatio et Paenitentia*, no. 35, p. 135.

[32] Cf. Alphonsus de Liguori, *Pratica del confessors per ben esercitare il suo ministero*, 1.2 (Modena: Tipografia Pontificia ed Arcivescovile "Immacolate Concezione," 1948), 3.

[33] See, for example, Origen, Homily 34.3, in *Origen: Homilies on Luke, Fragments on Luke*, trans., Joseph T. Lienhard (Washington, DC: Catholic University of America Press, 1996), 138; cf. also *New World Encyclopedia* contributors, "Parable of the Good Samaritan," *New World Encyclopedia*, accessed February 7, 2010, http://www.newworldencyclopedia.org/entry/Parable_of_the_Good_Samaritan?oldid=771732.

love and continues to this day in the loving care of the Church and its clergy, who received specific instructions to do everything necessary to bring about a full recovery. Christ's compassionate healing, in other words, continues in the Church and the ministry of her priests, who through their preaching, teaching, and administration of the sacraments, continue the healing of humanity's wounds until the end of time.

Priests, according to this interpretation of the parable, are called to be men of compassion, because Christ Himself was a man of compassion. If a priest is lacking in this basic Christian quality, then something has gone terribly wrong with his life and ministry. If he cannot "suffer with" others, how will he ever hope to follow in Christ's footsteps and "suffer for" them? A priest without compassion is a contradiction in terms. Such a person is not living the Gospel on a deep level of consciousness—and possibly not at all. As the priest and Levite in the parable, he seriously misunderstood the nature of his duties to God, his neighbors, and ultimately, himself.

As Saint John Vianney, a priest with compassion is a man of God and a true follower of Christ. He takes the time to be present to his people, to listen to their troubles, to suffer *with* them and, yes, at times, as we saw in the life of Maximilian Kolbe, even to suffer *for* them. He binds up their wounds, feeds them, and warms their hearts with a burning message of hope. He sees the face of the suffering Christ in the people he serves and knows that by ministering to them he is not only serving the Lord, but also being served by Him.

Most priests, I would venture to say, are to some degree both compassionate and compassionless. They strive to follow Jesus' example, that of the Good Samaritan, and yes, the Curé of Ars and Maximilian Kolbe, but all too often find that the priest and Levite of the parable are still very much alive in them. Most priests will admit there is a gap between the men of compassion they want to be and their actual lived experience. The question they must ask themselves is whether that gap between vision and reality is getting larger or smaller.

Let us pray that the gap continues to narrow. Let us pray that all priests will never cease asking and seeking to be compassionate, forgiving, and on fire with the love for Christ. Let us pray that the words of Saint Paul be ever on their lips: "Blessed be the God and Father of our Lord Jesus Christ, the Father of compassion and God of all encouragement, who encourages us in our every affliction, so that we may be able to encourage those who are in any affliction with the encouragement with which we ourselves are encouraged by God" (2 Cor 1:3-4). And again: "Now I rejoice in my sufferings for your sake, and in my flesh I am filling up what is lacking in the afflictions of Christ on behalf of his body, which is the church .... . For this I labor and struggle, in accord with the exercise of his power working within me" (Col 1:24, 29).

REFLECTION QUESTIONS

1. Why is compassion so important for the Catholic priesthood? What does it mean to "suffer with" others? What does it mean to "suffer for" others? How do priests show compassion in their ministry and daily lives? Is it possible for them to be too compassionate, too merciful, too forgiving? What can they do to allow Christ's compassion to shine through them with greater intensity?

2. What can priests do to narrow the gap between the compassion and the indifference in their lives and ministry? Is it simply a matter of asking Christ for help? Are there specific passages from Scripture and certain kinds of prayer that would be of particular help to them? What is the relationship between compassion and the Eucharist? In what way does a priest "suffer with" and "suffer for" others when he celebrates the sacraments?

3. Is there any connection between the priest as penitent and the priest as confessor? Does going to Confession regularly help a priest to be more compassionate in his dealings with others, especially when he hears their confessions? When hearing confessions, how can he be compassionate toward those who come to him and, at the same time, be just in his application of God's law? How can he balance being father, doctor, teacher, and judge?

4. Is there any connection between a priest's compassion and his experience of death? Can the loss of someone he loves—a parent, a brother, a sister, a friend—affect the way he deals with those who suffered similar losses? In what ways can his own experience of loss impact the way he visits someone who is dying, conduct

a wake service, or celebrate a Funeral Mass? How can his own experience of suffering help him to "suffer with" others?

SUGGESTED READINGS

Aschenbrenner, George A. *Quickening Fire in Our Midst: The Challenge of Diocesan Priestly Spirituality.* Chicago: Jesuit Way, 2002.

Dolan, Timothy M. *Priests for the Third Millennium.* Huntington, IN: Our Sunday Visitor, 2000.

Griffin, James A. *The Priestly Heart.* Staten Island, NY: Alba House, 1984.

Martini, Carlo Maria. *Some Years After: Reflections on the Ministry of the Priest.* Translated by Teresa Cadamartori. Dublin: Veritas, 1991.

McNeill, Donald P., Douglas A. Morrison, and Henri J. M. Nouwen. *Compassion: A Reflection on the Christian Life.* Garden City, NY: Image Books, 1983.

Power, Dermot. *A Spiritual Theology of the Priesthood: The Mystery of Christ and the Mission of the Priest.* Foreward by Robert Faricy. Edinburgh: T&T Clark, 1998.

Rahner, Karl. *The Priesthood.* Translated by Edward Quinn. New York: Herder and Herder, 1977.

Rigali, Justin. *I Call You Friends: The Priesthood—Merciful Love.* Chicago: Liturgical Training Publications, 2004.

Rossetti, Stephen J. *The Joy of the Priesthood.* Forward by Timothy M. Dolan. Notre Dame, IN: Ave Maria Press, 2005.

Smith, Karen Sue, ed. *Priesthood in the Modern World: A Reader.* Introduction by Philip J. Murnion. Franklin, WI: Sheed and Ward, 1999.

Chapter Five

MEN OF SERVICE:
PRIESTS AND THE PASTORAL LIFE

Rev. Anthony J. Costa, S.T.D.

Before the feast of Passover, Jesus knew that his hour had come to pass from this world to the Father. He loved his own in the world and he loved them to the end. The devil had already induced Judas, son of Simon the Iscariot, to hand him over. So, during supper, fully aware that the Father had put everything into his power and that he had come from God and was returning to God, he rose from supper and took off his outer garments. He took a towel and tied it around his waist. Then he poured water into a basin and began to wash the disciples' feet and dry them with the towel around his waist. He came to Simon Peter, who said to him, "Master, are you going to wash my feet?" Jesus answered and said to him, "What I am doing, you do not understand now, but you will understand later." Peter said to him, "You will never wash my feet." Jesus answered him, "Unless I wash you, you will have no inheritance with me." Simon Peter said to him, "Master, then not only my feet, but my hands and head as well." Jesus said to him, "Whoever has bathed has no need except to have his feet washed, for he is clean all over; so you are clean, but not all." For he knew who would betray him; for this reason, he said, "Not all of you are clean." So when he had washed their feet (and) put his garments back on and reclined at table again, he said to them, "Do you realize what I have done for you? You call me 'teacher' and 'master,' and rightly so, for indeed I am. If I, therefore, the master and teacher, have washed your feet, you ought to wash one another's feet. I have given you a model to follow, so that as I have done for you, you should also do (Jn 13:1-15).

Each year on Holy Thursday, the Church celebrates the evening Mass of the Lord's Supper to begin the Easter Triduum. The familiar text used is from the thirteenth chapter of the Gospel of John, with Jesus washing the feet of His disciples. In a powerful way this celebration commemorates the institution of the Eucharist, the institution of the priesthood, and Jesus' dramatic example of the meaning of loving service.

This presentation will first reflect upon the implications of Jesus' washing of the disciples' feet. We will then move to the Eucharist as the center of the pastoral life of the priest as a man of service. The role of prayer in his priesthood will be reviewed as an integral part of all aspects of ministry. Next, we will reflect on pastoral charity as the source of service, which leads into the gift of self as the way a priest follows the model of Jesus. Finally, examples of loving service will be summarized to highlight the various types and varieties of pastoral work.

IMPLICATIONS OF JESUS' WASHING OF THE DISCIPLES' FEET

The Gospel of John, like the Synoptic Gospels, indicates that Jesus shared a Last Supper with His closest followers. The Synoptics record the institution of the Eucharist at this meal within the context of the Passover celebration. The fourth Gospel, however, clearly notes that this meal was celebrated before the Passover (Jn 13:1). John does not record the institution at this time, but tells of a washing of the feet and then a sequence of farewell discourses from chapter thirteen through chapter seventeen. The washing of the feet is not reported in the Synoptics, but Luke includes a brief farewell discourse at the Last Supper (Lk 22:24-38). In this discourse Jesus tells the disciples that true greatness comes from service (Lk 22:24-30).

During the Johannine Last Supper, Jesus took a towel, poured water in a basin and became the servant who would wash the feet of the guest who had traveled the dusty roads of Israel. This act of humble service was a symbol of His love and concern for the disciples. Jesus gave them a model of service to follow in their relationships with others.

Pope John Paul II noted: "In the washing of feet Jesus reveals the depth of God's love for humanity: in Jesus, God places himself at the service of human beings! At the same time, he reveals the meaning of the Christian life."[1]

The disciples do not initially understand this action of Jesus at the Last Supper, but will comprehend the meaning later (Jn 13:7). Peter initially refused to participate in the washing until Jesus explained the consequences: "Unless I wash you, you will have no inheritance with me" (Jn 13:8). "The drama enacted by Jesus with the Twelve tells us that the Eucharist is so essential an act of the Christian life that without it one can have no share in Christ."[2] The true washing will come from Jesus' death when water and blood flow from His side (Jn 19:34). All followers are "washed clean" of sin in the waters of Baptism and will be nourished by the Body and Blood of Jesus.

In the Last Supper account of Luke, Jesus gave the command: "Do this in memory of me" (Lk 22:19). The words of Jesus in Paul's account, "Do this in remembrance of me" (1 Cor 11:24), are similar. The disciples are to celebrate this liturgical memorial instituted by Jesus in the future. Jesus gave a similar command after the washing of the feet (Jn 13:15): "I have given you a model to follow, so that as I have done for you, you should also do." The humble service of Jesus was to be repeated by His followers in the future. [3] The liturgical celebration and reception of the Eucharist was a regular occurrence by the end of the first century.[4] Jesus' act of service demonstrated the practical responsibility expected of those who received the Eucharist. The humble service of Jesus was to be imitated for all people.

---

[1] John Paul II, *Vita Consecrata*, no. 75.

[2] Aidan Nichols, *The Holy Eucharist: From the New Testament To Pope John Paul II* (Dublin: Veritas Publications, 1991), 17.

[3] Raniero Cantalamessa, *The Eucharist: Our Sanctification*, trans. Frances Lonergan Villa (Collegeville, MN: The Liturgical Press, 1993), 64-68.

[4] *Catechism of the Catholic Church*, nos. 1341-1343.

Jesus, the Master and Teacher, reversed the roles of the master and the servant by washing the feet of the disciples. The protest of Peter touched on how uncomfortable the disciples must have been with the implications of this action. An ongoing conversion was necessary to understand the meaning and follow through with the act of humble service. The source of love which enabled the disciples to respond in loving service to others was the Eucharist.

"Those who receive the body of the Lord and who open themselves to its spiritual influence, are transformed by it in such a way that they adopt the attitude of service and humble devotedness that inspired the institution of the Eucharist."[5] This is the command given to all disciples by way of their Baptism and a command to all priests uniquely by virtue of their ordination *in persona Christi*. It is the essence of what it means for the priest to be men of service.

Pope John Paul II provides the context for priestly service: "This ministerial priesthood which is our lot is also our vocation and our grace. It marks our whole life with the seal of the most necessary and most demanding of services, the salvation of souls."[6]

EUCHARIST

The Church encourages the daily celebration of the Eucharist as an essential part of the priest's spirituality.[7] This is the heart of his day from which all the other ministerial and personal activities will resonate. The priest is called to fully enter into this intimate encounter with Christ. He also leads the faithful in their participation of the celebration of the Mass. The *Directory on the Ministry and Life of Priests* summarizes this as follows:

> If the priest lends to Christ, Most Eternal High Priest, his intelligence, will, voice and hands so as to offer, through his very ministry, the sacramental sacrifice of redemption

---

[5] Jean Galot, *The Eucharist Heart*, trans. Aine Hayde (Dublin: Veritas Publications, 1990), 131.

[6] John Paul II, 1986 Holy Thursday Letter, no. 1, *Holy Thursday Letters: To My Brother Priests*, James P. Socias, ed. (Chicago: Midwest Theological Forum, 1992), 159-160.

[7] Second Vatican Council, *Presbyterorum Ordains*, nos. 5, 13.

to the Father, he should make his own the dispositions of the Master and, like Him, live those gifts for his brothers in the faith. He must therefore learn to unite himself intimately to the offering, placing his entire life upon the altar of sacrifice as a revealing sign of the gratuitous and anticipatory love of God.[8]

The pastoral ministry of the priest enables him to grow in holiness by encountering Jesus in the midst of apostolic work. The priest who celebrates the Eucharist is intimately united to God by the exercise of his ministry. He is able to make the vital connection between the complementarity of union with God at the altar and in apostolic work. Pope John Paul II reflected upon the example of Saint John Mary Vianney in the Holy Thursday Letter to Priests in 1986. "The eucharist was at the very center of his spiritual life and pastoral work. He said: 'All good works put together are not equivalent to the sacrifice of the Mass, because they are the works of men and the holy Mass is the work of God.'"[9]

The priest's celebration of the Mass naturally leads to adoration of the Blessed Sacrament. The praise offered to God throughout the day has its source in the Mass. This prayer is essential for priestly spirituality. The Congregation for the Clergy's *Directory on the Ministry and Life of Priests* notes:

> It is hoped that the priests entrusted with the guidance of communities dedicate long periods of time for communal adoration and reserve the greatest attention and honor for the Most Blessed Sacrament of the altar, also outside of Holy Mass, over any other rite or gesture.[10]

We have the inspiration of saints such as Katharine Drexel, whose time in the presence of the Blessed Sacrament was not simply for her benefit, but also for those she encountered in the apostolic work. In

---

[8] Congregation for the Clergy, *Directory on the Ministry and Life of Priests*, no. 48.

[9] John Paul II, 1986 Holy Thursday Letter, no. 8, *Holy Thursday Letters*, 165.

[10] Congregation for the Clergy, *Directory on the Ministry and Life of Priests*, no. 50.

a similar way, the intimate time with Our Lord in adoration provides fruits the priest then shares with others in his ministry.

By imitating the mystery of the Eucharist celebrated at Mass, the priest empties himself in order to serve. The Eucharist reveals the pride and self-love that keeps him from dying to sin to live in Christ. This encounter leads to conversion and a desire to touch others with the healing of Jesus. Pope John Paul II spoke of the intimate connection between the celebration of the Mass and the pastoral service that flows from the Eucharist into the life and ministry of the priest:

> The grace and the charity of the altar thus extends to the pulpit, to the confessional, to the parish activities, to the school, to the oratory, to the houses and to the streets, to the hospitals, to the means of transport and those of social communication, everywhere the presbyter has the possibility of fulfilling his duties as a shepherd: in every instance it is his Mass which expands itself, it is his spiritual union with Christ the Priest and Victim who leads him to be—as Saint Ignatius of Antioch used to say—"wheat of God to be made the purest bread for Christ"—for the good of the brethren.[11]

PRAYER

Saint Teresa of Avila is the great doctor of the Church for articulating the grades of prayer. Her inspiring work, *The Interior Castle*, provides insights on prayer and activity that are practical for everyone and resonate in a special way for the priest as a man of service. Saint Teresa clearly makes the connection with love of God and love of others, as one moves through the mansions—or dwelling places— of the castle, as an image of coming into a deeper union with God.

She notes that love should not be idle. In the Fifth Dwelling Places, the prayer of union, Saint Teresa affirms that one so intimate with God must walk with special care and attentiveness to the exercise of virtue, with particular emphasis on love of neighbor, humility, and the faithful performance of ordinary tasks. She presents in the

---

[11] John Paul II, Catechesis at the "General Audience," no. 7, July 7, 1993, at the Vatican (translated from the Italian).

Seventh Dwelling Places, the point of ecstatic prayer, the image of the spiritual marriage of the soul with God. She concludes here that the purpose of all these splendid favors bestowed by God is that one might live as Christ and that the fruit of the spiritual marriage must be good works.

The *Decree on the Ministry and Life of Priests* from the Second Vatican council summarizes the connection between prayer and pastoral ministry as an integral part of the spirituality of the priest: "By the sacred actions which are theirs daily as well as by their entire ministry which they share with the bishop and their fellow priests, they are directed to perfection in their lives."[12] The spiritual life of the priest is deepened through his apostolic work, motivated by love of God. In the Post-Synodal Apostolic Exhortation of Pope John Paul II, *Pastores Dabo Vobis*, we read, "The relation of the priest to Jesus Christ, and in him to his Church, is found in the very being of the priest by virtue of his sacramental consecration/anointing and in his activity, that is, in his mission or ministry."[13] Work done in loving service for God and others nurture the priest's relationship with Jesus through an intimate participation in His ministry. Again in *Pastores Dabo Vobis* we read: "It is above all in the celebration of the sacraments and in the celebration of the Liturgy of the Hours that the priest is called to live and witness to the deep unity between the exercise of his ministry and his spiritual life."[14] The integration of prayer and pastoral work enable the priest to participate in the Paschal Mystery throughout the day.

The *Code of Canon Law* links the pastoral ministry and sanctification with the spiritual formation of seminarians. This is also an integral part of the continuing spiritual growth of the priest.

> Through their spiritual formation, the students are to become equipped to exercise fruitfully the pastoral ministry and they are to be formed in a missionary spirit; in the course of their formation they are to learn that a

---

[12] Second Vatican Council, *Presbyterorum Ordinis*, no. 12.

[13] John Paul II, *Pastores Dabo Vobis*, no. 16.

[14] Ibid., no. 26.

ministry which is always carried out in living faith and in charity fosters their own sanctity.[15]

In the midst of many challenging and diverse pastoral responsibilities, a priest must be rooted as a man of prayer. How often have we read from the saints or heard from a retreat master that you cannot give what you do not have? We encountered this reality many times in our own priesthood. Sadly, we saw the results of not having a healthy spiritual life in the eyes of a brother priest who was active about many things, but experiences emptiness in his ministry. In a talk to the clergy in Germany, Pope Benedict XVI gave all priests a great challenge.

> Generous self-giving for others is impossible without discipline and constant recovery of true faith-filled interiority. The effectiveness of pastoral action depends, ultimately, upon prayer; otherwise, service becomes empty activism. Therefore the time spent in direct encounter with God in prayer can rightly be described as the pastoral priority par excellence: It is the soul's breath, without which the priest necessarily remains "breathless," deprived of the "oxygen" of optimism and joy, which he needs if he is to allow himself to be sent, day by day, as a worker into the Lord's harvest.[16]

Saint Catherine of Siena has a powerful image for one to be united with Christ in prayer. The image involves receiving the life-giving waters needed for service. There is a fountain that contains this water, and the individual has a pitcher to collect the precious nourishment. The loving service involves pouring out the water from the pitcher into the cups of those who are served. One way of operating is to empty the pitcher and then return to the fountain for more water. This, however, is precisely what she wants us to avoid doing in our daily work and ministry. The way of humble service depending upon God involves holding a second pitcher in the other hand. One

---

[15] *Code of Canon Law: Latin–English Edition*, can. 245, trans. The Canon Law Society of America (Washington, D.C.: Canon Law Society of America, 1983), 82-85.

[16] Benedict XVI, The Pope's Prepared Text for Clergy of Freising, September 14, 2006.

needs to be constantly nourished with the life giving waters while pouring out the other pitcher in service.

An image for prayer and the pastoral life that Saint Catherine of Siena might use today is a car. We fill up with gas and then drive the car around while being attentive to when the gas gauge is nearing empty. At that point we return to the gas station to fill the tank and then begin the process of driving from place to place. This works fine for a car, but is disastrous for the spiritual life and pastoral service of the priest. Pope John Paul II wrote of the foundation of prayer for the priest.

> As sharers in the priesthood of Christ, which is inseparably connected with His sacrifice, we too must place at the foundation of our priestly existence the cornerstone of prayer. It will enable us to harmonize our lives with our priestly service, preserving intact the *identity and authenticity* of this vocation, which has become our special inheritance in the Church, as the community of the People of God.[17]

The prayer of Jesus is witnessed extensively in the four Gospels intimately related to His life and public ministry. In reading the following list of Scriptural citations, consider how the priest is called to be a man of prayer in his life and ministry.

- when His mission is revealed by the Father (Lk 3:21-22)
- before He calls the Apostles (Lk 6:12)
- when He blesses God at the multiplication of the loaves (Mt 14:19; 15:36; Mk 6:41; 8:7; Lk 9:16; Jn 6:11)
- when he is transfigured on the mountain (Lk 9:28-29)
- when he heals the deaf mute (Mk 7:34)
- when he raises Lazarus (Jn 11:41ff.)
- before he asks for Peter's confession of faith (Lk 9:18)
- when he teaches the disciples how to pray (Lk 11:1)
- when his disciples return from their mission (Mt 11:25ff.)
- when he blesses the little children (Mt 19:13)
- when he prays for Peter (Lk 22:32)
- he would retire into the desert or into the hills to pray (Mk 1:35; 6:46; Lk 5:16; see Mt 4:1 and parallels; Mt 14:23)

---

[17] John Paul II, 1987 Holy Thursday Letter, no. 10, *Holy Thursday Letters*, 183.

- rising very early (Mk 1:35)
- spending the night as far as the fourth watch (Mt 14:23, 25; Mk 6:46, 48)
- in prayer to God (Lk 6:12)
- in the synagogues, which he entered on the Sabbath "as his custom was" (Lk 4:16)
- in the temple which he called a house of prayer (Mt 21:31 and parallels)
- the Last Supper (Mt 26:26 and parallels)
- the meal at Emmaus (Lk 24:30)
- in a hymn of praise (Mt 26:30 and parallels)
- as his passion was approaching (Jn 12:27ff.)
- in the agony in the Garden (Mt 26:36-44 and parallels)
- on the Cross (Luke 23:34, 46; Mt 27:46; Mk 15:34)[18]

Prayer was not an interruption in His routine, but was an integral part of His whole mission. The Gospel of Luke gives special attention to the prayer of Jesus. While the Gospel of Mark includes the fact that Jesus prayed at key moments in his public life, Luke's Gospel reflects that Jesus conducted His whole life in an atmosphere of prayer.[19]

The priest's model of prayer in ministry and service of others is focused upon the example of Jesus. "St. John Mary Vianney did not content himself with the ritual carrying out of the activities of his ministry. It was his heart and his life which he sought to conform to Christ."[20]

Prayer enables the priest to be sensitive to the various and diverse needs of those he serves in our modern world. We share in the mission of the Good Shepherd, who is lovingly attentive to those entrusted to his care. The children in kindergarten, young people in secondary school, adults, and the senior citizens are all part of his flock. He knows that special attention needs to be given to the sick and dying. Those who are suffering had a prominent place in the public ministry of Jesus. The priest must be present to support married life and

---

[18] Cf. *The General Instruction of the Liturgy of the Hours*, no. 4.

[19] John Sheets, S. J., *The Spirit Speaks In Us* (Denville, NJ: Dimension Books, 1968), 25.

[20] John Paul II, 1986 Holy Thursday Letter, no. 11, *Holy Thursday Letters*, 168.

families in every way possible. He desires to promote vocations to the priesthood and religious life among those he encounters in daily living. He walks the road to recovery along with the man or woman overcoming an addiction. He also encounters those who reject his offer of assistance and at times faces the anger of someone who was hurt in the past. The priest is present in all the critical moments of the lives of others.

We know the reality: The needs of the flock continue to increase, while the number of priests who are available to serve has declined. It can be overwhelming for the priest to recognize all the needs and be unable to meet them. He must prayerfully and humbly be sensitive to where God is calling him to be and generously respond. This discernment is the way of the Father and leads to the sanctification of both those who are being served along with the priest himself.

There are particular aspects of pastoral service that he readily accepts and those that are more challenging based upon his disposition and temperament. A priest may zealously climb a ladder to examine the progress of the installation of a new roof, but dread the upcoming finance meeting that evening. The discernment is being where God is directing him to serve in a unique way.

With the limitations of time, energy, and resources, there can be the temptation to have a "one size fits all" approach to pastoral concerns. Adrienne von Speyr gives an insightful reflection on the importance of prayerfully approaching how the priest is invited to serve the individual based upon their specific needs, rather than having a programmed response. This way of priestly service requires a man of prayer intimately united to Jesus.

> People's concerns are always unique to them; for him they become more and more the same, and it would seem natural to divide them into categories and have a handy prescription for each one. But that is precisely what he must not do. He must lead each one to the Lord personally ... Even before he learns of the pastoral situations which a priest can encounter, he must become acquainted with the Lord's approach and must contemplate it without having any particular application in mind. If he has this prior and

general knowledge of Christ's care of souls, he will be able to solve the individual pastoral problem in its light.[21]

CHARITY

The priest strives for the perfection of charity, as in the case of the spirituality of the laity and consecrated life. He is called to share in the pastoral charity of Jesus through the sacrament of Holy Orders. Pope John Paul II specifically notes the gift of pastoral charity in *Pastores Dabo Vobis.*

> The internal principle, the force which animates and guides the spiritual life of the priest inasmuch as he is configured to Christ the Head and Shepherd, is pastoral charity, as a participation in Jesus Christ's own pastoral charity, a gift freely bestowed by the Holy Spirit and likewise a task and a call which demand a free and committed response on the part of the priest.[22]

Jesus expressed the meaning of pastoral charity by His complete self-giving in the Eucharist. The priest must express his gift of self in loving service modeled on the example of Jesus. The source of pastoral charity in the life of the priest is the Eucharistic sacrifice. The *Decree on the Ministry and Life of Priests* refers to a priestly soul. "This pastoral charity flows out in a very special way from the Eucharistic sacrifice. This stands as the root and center of the whole life of a priest. What takes place on the altar of sacrifice, the priestly heart must make his own. This cannot be done unless priests through prayer continue to penetrate more deeply into the mystery of Christ."[23] The priest offers the sacrifice of the Mass and enters into sacrificial apostolic work in service of God and others through pastoral charity.

Pastoral charity integrates the spiritual life of the priest by uniting many diverse ministerial activities. The priest's need for personal prayer and responsibility to pray for the Church is a priority among

---

[21] Adrienne von Speyr, *The World of Prayer* (San Francisco: Ignatius Press, 1985), 176-177.

[22] John Paul II, *Pastores Dabo Vobis*, no. 23.

[23] Second Vatican Council, *Presbyterorum Ordinis*, no. 14.

the many apostolic obligations faced each day. *Pastores Dabo Vobis* provides a clear insight on the necessity of integration in the life of the priest. "Only by directing every moment and every one of his acts toward the fundamental choice to 'give his life for the flock' can the priest guarantee this unity which is vital and indispensable for his harmony and spiritual balance."[24]

God does not attach any encumbrances to the complete gift of His unconditional love. The Father loved the world so much that He gave His only Son for humanity to have life (Jn 3:16). The Son offered Himself completely to the Father in loving obedience on the Cross (Phil 2:6-11). Our response to this unconditional love is one of thanksgiving, which draws us closer into the life of the Trinity. Union with the Trinity develops into a growing inclination to offer thanks to God. Galot challenges us on the full meaning of thanksgiving. "For the Christian, as for Jesus, thanksgiving is not limited to saying 'thank you' to the Father. It implies the will to give him back as much as possible of what he has given and, consequently, a personal offering."[25]

Charitable works of the Christian community signify the presence of God's love in the world. The Second Vatican Council's *Decree on the Church's Missionary Activity* points to the apostolate of the priest: "[B]y reason of the eucharistic sacrifice, this community is ceaselessly on the way with Christ to the Father; carefully nourished on the word of God it bears witness to Christ; and finally, it walks in charity and is fervent with the apostolic spirit."[26] The Eucharist enables our love of God to extend to a love of others. The loving service given to others, however, does not eliminate our responsibility to give thanks to God Himself. The faithful must follow the example of Jesus, who was foremost the Servant of God and then the Servant of mankind.

The *Catechism of the Catholic Church* summarizes the implications of priestly service.

> "The grace of the Lord Jesus Christ and the love of God and the fellowship of the Holy Spirit" (2 Cor 13:13) have to remain with us always and bear fruit beyond

---

[24] John Paul II, *Pastores Dabo Vobis*, no. 23.

[25] Galot, *The Eucharist Heart*, 85.

[26] Second Vatican Council, *Ad Gentes*, no. 15.

the Eucharistic celebration. The Church therefore asks the Father to send the Holy Spirit to make the lives of the faithful a living sacrifice to God by their spiritual transformation into the image of Christ, by concern for the Church's unity, and by taking part in her mission through the witness and service of charity.[27]

The celebration of the Eucharist "should lead to various works of charity and mutual help, as well as to missionary activity and to different forms of Christian witness."[28] Jesus was drawn to the poor and sick during His public ministry and brought healing of body and spirit. He wanted all people to share in His abundant life and love in union with the Father. Jesus fed the material needs of the crowds in the multiplication of the loaves and fishes, but pointed to the true food of the Eucharist for everlasting life. He invites us to share in His mission of feeding and liberating the poor. The *Dogmatic Constitution on the Church* from the Second Vatican Council gives an insight to the sacramental ministry of the priest: "[B]y the sacraments, especially the Holy Eucharist, that charity toward God and man which is the soul of the apostolate is communicated and nourished."[29] Jesus' concern for the poor was an integral part of the ministry of the apostolic Church (Gal 2:10). Authentic participation in the celebration of the Eucharist leads to charity for others, especially the needy, in loving service.

GIFT OF SELF

Pastores Dabo Vobis summarizes the oblation of Jesus as follows: "Jesus Christ, who brought his pastoral charity to perfection on the cross with a complete exterior and interior emptying of self, is both the model and source of the virtues of obedience, chastity and poverty which the priest is called to live out . . ."[30] The complete self-offering of Jesus to the Father is the pattern for the life of the priest. He makes a free choice to offer himself to God in loving service of

---

[27] *Catechism of the Catholic Church*, no. 1109.

[28] Second Vatican Council, *Presbyterorum Ordinis,* no. 6.

[29] Second Vatican Council, *Lumen Gentium,* no. 33.

[30] John Paul II, *Pastores Dabo Vobis,* 30.

others for the proclamation of the Gospel to all. Jesus revealed the full implications of the priesthood during His earthly life and especially through His passion, death, and resurrection. The priesthood of Jesus Christ is rooted in the Cross. Those who share in His priesthood must embrace the Cross by the emptying of self in service of God and others.

Father Thomas Acklin notes the intimate connection between the offering of Jesus and the offering of the priest in our modern world.

> What is needed in the church today is a priesthood of servant hearts, unafraid of power yet not intoxicated by it—servant hearts authorized in their priesthood by the servant heart of Jesus Christ. Like Jesus, ordained priests must be meek and humble of heart; they must not be afraid to be consumed in self-gift through the self-gift of Jesus Christ, who has called them to follow Him more closely.[31]

We normally hear about the extraordinary service of a priest in the course of his pastoral ministry. An example is his presence with the parents and family whose child was killed in a tragic car accident and the consoling homily at the funeral. Another example is his creativity and administrative skills when the new church is constructed. Events such as these are draining, and represent what the gift of self means in a practical way for the priest.

Everyday events are often hidden; however, they are the meat and potatoes of the priest's pastoral service. It is here that the emptying of self in service of God and others is motivated by love. He is available at all hours of the day to meet the person in the rectory who wants to see a priest for Confession. It means driving an hour to visit a long time parishioner who generously gave herself to the parish and now lives in a nursing home. He is present, when the schedule allows, for the Boy Scout banquet, parish sporting events, Sodality devotions, and Senior Citizen luncheons because it means so much to his parishioners to know he supports their efforts. On some days, perhaps every day depending on the circumstances of the parish, he will open the church each morning.

---

[31] Thomas Acklin, *The Unchanging Heart of the Priesthood* (Steubenville, OH: Emmaus Road, 2005), 52.

All these various activities require precious time and energy and involve a gift of self. Saint Paul gives us the powerful image of being poured out as a libation in service to others. In the present culture, which idolizes power and wealth, the humble service of Christ can be discounted and even utterly ridiculed. The complicated situations of family life today present challenges that could not be contemplated by the priest while in formation as a seminarian. Priestly service is always costly because it means embracing the Cross and following Jesus to Calvary. We trust that He provides the grace required for the day and respond by working faithfully and diligently. We know the cost of discipleship and pray to be motivated in our pastoral service in our love for God manifested in our love for others.

A great blessing and support for us is the fraternity we share in every aspect of our ministerial priesthood. We can talk with our brother priests when discerning how to respond to a situation we have not encountered before in pastoral ministry. It is amazing how a priest ordained for many years can still say, "I have never seen this one before." The technological advancements in medical moral issues, for example, can seem overwhelming when counseling a family at a sensitive time in their lives. Knowing that assistance is only a phone call away is a tremendous consolation as we minister to others.

The commitment of the priest as a man of service has a cost, and we know this on the day of our ordination. We reaffirm this commitment each year at the Chrism Mass, united with the bishop and the faithful of the diocese. The priest follows the model of Jesus in giving Himself fully and completely in loving service of others. We have the inspiring example of priesthood from saints such as John Vianney. "The priest must always be ready to respond to the needs of souls," said the Curé of Ars. "He is not for himself, he is for you."[32]

TYPES OF SERVICE

The clergy at a diocesan day of recollection were challenged with a direct statement made by the priest conducting the recollection. "If you ever find yourself saying, 'I was not ordained for this,' stop immediately and say, 'oh, yes I was.'" The statement is simple; yet it

[32] John Paul II, 1986 Holy Thursday Letter, no. 10, *Holy Thursday Letters*, 168.

resonates considering all the various ways that a priest serves. The priest's ministry is impacted by the needs of the community he serves in a concrete place and time. An assignment in the inner city will pose different challenges than an assignment to hospital ministry. The common thread to the many apostolic works is the same mission to preach the Gospel.

The identity of the priest must be clearly understood by the man and the community he serves. He does many different things, but the activity does not define who he is as a priest of Jesus Christ and an ordained minister of the Church. There will be confusion and dis-illusionment if a priest sees himself solely in terms of activity. It is sad to hear a pastor say that he is not effective because enrollment in the parish school continues to decline. It is also sad to have a priest think he is doing all that is expected because the bills are paid while he has not taken a real retreat in five years. Father George Aschenbrenner provides a concise description of the identity of the priest in his book on the challenge of diocesan priestly spirituality.

> The priest's identity is in God's love alone, faithful from the first moment of the priest's creation and continuing into the fullness of eternal life. This faithful love of God takes most dramatic expression in Jesus' death for him on the cross. This, beyond anyone or anything else, establishes the priest's identity as one who is loved. Living in the light of this loved identity provides an anchor against the tides of ambition.[33]

A woman who was a consecrated religious and a doctor was once asked about homilies. What was the most important message people should hear? Her answer, which fills the pages of Sacred Scripture, was striking—people need to hear that God loves them.

She is right. We all need to be rooted in the lived experience of being loved by God because we are His children. This is true for the child in school, the woman working at the store, the married couple, and the priest. It is particularly important for the priest to know this at the very core of his being, because he must authentically convey this to others in words and actions. We can slip and act as though we are loved by God simply because of what we do.

---

[33] George Aschenbrenner, *Quickening the Fire In Our Midst: The Challenge of Diocesan Priestly Spirituality* (Loyola Press: Chicago, 2002), 56.

A priest who knows he is loved has the interior freedom to discern what God is asking of him and respond in love. The critical aspect is to be faithful to be where God is guiding, and not simply to set one's own agenda. This sounds clear enough on a calm day, but when five requests are sitting on the desk and only one or two can be accepted, it is another story. To use Father Aschenbrenner's words, it can be a period when the "tides of ambition" begin to flow. At this point we must humbly be sensitive to the Lord.

Saint Ignatius of Loyola provides a guide for everyone in the principle and foundation of the Spiritual Exercises. He gives priests a standard to guide their pastoral ministry in the humble way of discipleship.

> Human beings are created to praise, reverence, and serve God Our Lord, and by means of doing this to save their souls.

> The other things on the face of the earth are created for the human beings, to help them in the pursuit of the end for which they are created.

> From this it follows that we ought to use these things to the extent that they help us toward our end, and free ourselves from them to the extent that they hinder us from it.

> To attain this it is necessary to make ourselves indifferent to all created things, in regard to everything which is left to our free will and is not forbidden. Consequently, on our own part we ought not to seek health rather than sickness, wealth rather than poverty, honor rather than dishonor, a long life rather than a short one, and so on in all other matters.

> Rather, we ought to desire and choose only that which is more conducive to the end for which we are created.[34]

The "end" for which we are created is the "pearl of great price." This parable of Jesus invites us to sell everything in order to obtain this precious gift. Losing a sense of the primacy of God's love can make seeking "honor rather than dishonor" more important than

---

[34] George Ganss, S.J., trans. and comm., *The Spiritual Exercises of Saint Ignatius* (Chicago, IL: Loyola Press, 1992), 32.

Him. Saint Ignatius invites us to the freedom of service as priests doing the will of the Father.

We are each called in a unique and special way to living the glory of God. A movie called *Chariots of Fire* was popular in the 1980s. The setting was focused around preparation for the summer Olympic Games. One of the characters was a man who desired to be a missionary in China. He was also a runner representing Great Britain in training for the Olympics and it was taking a substantial amount of his time and energy. His sister confronted him about the running and expressed concern that it was distracting him from becoming a missionary. His response was memorable. "I know God made me for a purpose, but He also made me fast. When I run I can feel His glory." When we are faithful to what God is asking of us, we too can feel His glory.

A certain amount of the priest's ministry is crafted by virtue of the particular assignment. The priest will be called to preach, teach, and sanctify in caring for the people entrusted to his care. There will be administrative work, including finances and supervising employees. Each assignment, however, will have a unique blend depending upon the needs of the community. The sacramental ministry in a large suburban parish will require more time than that of an older parish in the city. A priest who is serving in the teaching apostolate will be investing himself in education and formation. The hospital chaplain will be serving the needs of the sick and bringing the consolation of Christ's peace to the patients and their families.

There is also flexibility in each assignment where the priest must discern how God is inviting him to serve. On any given day there will be several places where he can be ministering, but only one can be chosen. There may be an opportunity to see the children in the school, visit parishioners in a local hospital, or to check in with the man who recently moved into a nursing home. In an ideal setting all of these could be accomplished, but in reality this is not possible, given time constraints and other responsibilities. At this point, discernment must be made to see where God is leading, rather than simply choosing the one that is more appealing or comfortable. This is where the prayerful disposition of the priest will enable him to be sensitive to the guiding hand of the Lord.

Saint Ignatius of Loyola crafted a prayerful way of discerning where God is directing us. Father Aschenbrenner developed a *Consciousness Examen* based upon a part of the Spiritual Exercises of Saint Ignatius. This examen primarily assists the priest, and all people, in being sensitive to the subtle, intimate, affective ways in which God dealt with us over the past day or even the past few hours. We can then assess if our actions were responses to the promptings of the Holy Spirit.[35] In this way we can recognize more clearly how God is speaking to us in the future and respond in love.

As we conclude our reflections on the priest as a man of service, we look to the example of Saint John Mary Vianney as cited by Pope John Paul II. In this Year for Priests, may we all be more centered in the loving service rooted in the heart of Christ.

> Dear brother priests, nourished by the Second Vatican Council which has felicitously placed the priest's consecration within the framework of his pastoral mission, let us join St. John Mary Vianney and seek the dynamism of our pastoral zeal in the heart of Jesus, in his love for souls. If we do not draw from the same source, our ministry risks bearing little fruit!

REFLECTION QUESTIONS

1. How is the Eucharist the center of a priest's pastoral ministry? How is it the center of your ministry? How does the prayer of Jesus influence the priest's integration of contemplation and service?

2. Pope John Paul II called pastoral charity a gift of the Holy Spirit and a call which demands a free and committed response by the priest. What are the practical implications for you? How does the model of Jesus washing the feet of the disciples provide an insight for the priest?

3. How does the priest embrace the Cross in his daily ministry of service? In what ways does a priest balance the total giving of self and still maintain his overall health and wellness?

---

[35] Aschenbrenner, *Quickening the Fire In Our Midst*, 170-177.

4. What areas of service do you find most rewarding? Most challenging? On any given day it is impossible to meet all of the potential needs of pastoral ministry. How do you prayerfully discern where God is guiding you to serve on that particular day?

SUGGESTED READINGS

Acklin, Thomas. *The Unchanging Heart of the Priesthood: A Faith Perspective on the Mystery and the Reality of Priesthood in the Church.* Steubenville, OH: Emmaus Road Pub., 2005.

Aschenbrenner, George A. *Quickening the Fire in Our Midst: The Challenge of Diocesan Priestly Spirituality.* Chicago: Loyola Press, 2002.

Benedict XVI, Pope. The Pope's Prepared Text for Clergy of Freising. September 14, 2006. Accessed May 7, 2010. http://www.yourcatholicvoice.org/insight.php?article=3641.

Cantalamessa, Raniero. *The Eucharist: Our Sanctification*, Frances Lonergan Villa, trans. Collegeville, MN: The Liturgical Press, 1993.

Coleman, Gerald D. *Catholic Priesthood: Formation and Human Development.* Liguori, MO: Liguori Publications, 2006.

Congregation for the Clergy. *Directory on the Ministry and Life of Priests.* United States Catholic Conference: Libreria Editrice Vaticana, 1994.

Congregation for the Doctrine of the Faith. *From "Inter Insigniores" to "Ordinatio Sacerdotatalis": Documents and Commentaries* [FIIOS]. Washington DC: United States Catholic Conference, 1998.

Galot, Jean. *The Eucharist Heart.* Aine Hayde, trans. Dublin: Veritas Publications, 1990.

John Paul II, Pope. *Letters to My Brother Priests.* Chicago: Midwest Theological Forum, 1992.

Nichols, Aidan. *The Holy Eucharist: From the New Testament to Pope John Paul II.* Dublin: Veritas Publications, 1991.

Chapter Six

MEN OF VISION:
PRIESTS AND LEADERSHIP

Rev. Msgr. David E. Diamond, Ph.D.

This evening I find myself in the unique position of speaking last in this series on priesthood, with the topic being "Men of Vision: Priests and Leadership." It is rather like a batter coming to his turn at the plate when his five teammates already hit home runs—not that I feel any pressure. The previous presentations were marked by clarity and scholarship to which I can only hope to add through my efforts tonight.

I believe it is more than appropriate to begin this lecture on priests and leadership this evening with a story of the beginning of Saint John Vianney's own work as leader of the parish of Ars. The story is told of Saint John Vianney's approach to his assignment in the city of Ars. It was late in the day and with the sun setting, he pushed a cart filled with his belongings along a country lane. He came upon a boy, to whom he asked, how far it was to Ars. The boy pointed to the city in the distance; seeing it, Vianney knelt to pray. Upon arising, the boy accompanied him to the church. At that time Vianney said to him: You have shown me the way to Ars—now I will show you the way to heaven. My presentation tonight is about the means by which a priest can fulfill that task which all priests share: providing leadership, leading people to heaven.

RESEARCH ON LEADERSHIP

The issue of leadership has long been an interest of thinkers and writers as well as leaders. However, leadership as a distinct entity has only recently been the focus of academic research. Researchers, theorists, philosophers, and scientists dealt with the issue literally for centuries, but formal exploration of what makes a leader has only been around since about the middle of the twentieth century. Up until about the middle of the nineteenth century, if they thought about it at all, people generally accepted the Aristotelian understanding of leadership as being a matter of birth. An Englishman named Francis Galton changed that when he began investigating characteristics of people in order to categorize them. On the basis of Galton's writing in the 1800s, those who studied leaders and leadership gave their attention to the personal attributes of the leader, i.e., his or her traits.[1]

For the most part, there was a general acceptance and a sort of benign misapplication of the Shakespearean admonition: "Be not afraid of greatness: some are born great, some achieve greatness, and some have greatness thrust upon them."[2] This mindset was typified in the understanding of leadership in terms of traits, or characteristics, as well as circumstances in which people find themselves. Some believe that fate managed a way to fashion an opportunity for an individual's abilities to shine forth.

There was a shift in this type of thought when researchers began to focus not so much on the personal traits that a leader possessed, as much as linking a skill set to a situation. This framework provided the means to examine leadership within a determined area of human endeavor and explore those skills which leaders are able to manifest. If you are a fan of history, you may be of a mind to think the right leaders seem to emerge by necessity at a dynamic or critical time in history. The right person seems to come along at the right time. There is some evidence to support that assertion: Churchill and FDR of the twentieth century; Lincoln in the middle of the 1800s; Washington, Adams and Franklin at the beginning of our nation's history. While this type of thinking may be acceptable for an armchair historian, for those charged with specific tasks in relation to forming leaders, and specifically priests, mere circumstance or skills cannot simply be left to the genetic roll of the dice or the happenstance of history.

---

[1] Wayne K. Hoy, and Cecil G. Miskel, *Educational Administration: Theory, Research, Practice* (New York: McGraw Hill, Inc., 1991).

[2] William Shakespeare, *Twelfth Night*, Act II, Scene V, 156-159.

Two areas where recent investigation into leadership has gained tremendous momentum are business and education. In the arena of business, we moved far away from Dale Carnegie's book, *How to Win Friends and Influence People*. There are now all kinds of publications available to "guarantee" a person's ability to become an effective leader. We have a sampling of this from one author, Stephen Covey:

The 7 Habits of Highly Effective People;

The 7 Habits of Highly Effective People: Personal Workbook;

The 7 Habits Of Highly Effective Teens;

This next one has the remarkably redundant title of *Daily Reflections for Highly Effective People: Living the 7 Habits of Highly Effective People Every Day*;

The 7 Habits of Highly Effective Network Marketing Professionals;

Finally, my personal favorite: *The 7 Habits of Highly Effective People (Simplified Chinese Version)*.

People seek to be leaders and they seek leadership in a variety of ways. This was humorously shown in the Broadway musical *How to Succeed in Business Without Really Trying*. While the flaws and foibles of the characters in that show proved amusing, the humor was ironic. The ambitious individual in a corporate setting, who manipulates situations and people for his own gain, was quite close to reality. Remove the music and tap dancing, and I suspect you will find more than a shadow of resemblance to the contemporary corporation. I am told that the latest incarnation of this type of presentation is in the popular television show *Mad Men,* which is a retro-presentation of the 1960s and the ruthlessly ambitious men of an advertising company whose sole creed is self promotion.

There are a variety of theories of leadership that emerged as being acceptable, even desirable, in both business and education. Yet, there is another type of leadership that is much more akin to the leadership of a Catholic priest. I will briefly touch on some popular models of leadership, and then ultimately focus on the leadership that a priest provides, not as a mere extension of the leadership that takes place in the corporate world or the academy, but the leadership that is unique to being a priest. After that, I will explore that aspect of priesthood marked by prophetic leadership, and conclude with those specific aspects of priestly leadership given to us by our Lord.

TRANSFORMATIONAL V. TRANSACTIONAL LEADERSHIP

In the early '80s, educational researchers established a kind of rallying cry for the reshaping of schools in the United States.[3] The call for this re-configuration led writers to examine the impact that a style of leadership known as "transformational" has on an organization. As I describe aspects of transformational, or transformative leadership, I encourage you to think of a person you recognize as a leader: Pope John Paul II or Pope Benedict, a leader in your religious community, a priest you know in a parish setting. In these people you may or may not find aspects of these models. However, I suspect that one will be more readily recognized than another.

Transformational leadership is a process in which leaders and followers raise one another to higher levels of morality and motivation.

> The transforming leader recognizes an existing need or demand of a potential follower. But beyond that, the transforming leader looks for potential motives in followers, seeks to satisfy higher needs, and engages the full person of the follower. The result of the transforming leadership is a relationship ... that converts followers into leaders and may convert leaders into moral agents.[4]

Unlike the trait theory of leadership, based on the unique aspects of one's personality or even physiology, or the situational theory, based on the context within which the leader's behavior occurs,

---

[3] Thomas Sergiovanni, *The New School Executive: A Theory of Administration* (New York: Dodd, Mead, and Company, 1973); R. Edmonds, "Effective Schools for the Urban Poor," *Educational Leadership*, 37 (1979): 15-18, 20-24; Kenneth Leithwood, "Transformational Leadership and School Restructuring" (Paper presented at the Annual Meeting of the International Congress for School Effectiveness and Improvement, Victoria, British Columbia, Canada, 1992); Lawrence Lezotte, "The Nexus of Instructional Leadership and Effective Schools," *School Administrator*, 51 (1994): 20-33.

[4] James M. Burns, *Leadership* (New York: Harper and Row, 1978), 4.

transformational leadership is a process, not simply a set of actions. The transformational leader seeks to raise the consciousness of followers by appealing to higher ideals and moral values.[5]

By its nature, the process of consciousness-raising in a transformational relationship presumes reciprocity among the members. The leader and the subordinate can influence each other. The transformational leader seeks to influence the members of an organization by appealing to moral virtues and ideals, which the members of the organization share.[6]

Transformational leadership can be exhibited by anyone in the organization, no matter what position he or she holds. Transformational leadership is, I believe, spiritual at its center because in many ways it empowers people to move beyond what they thought themselves capable of doing and being, and they move to a greater manifestation of abilities. Is that not what priests are called to do: Bring God to men and men to God.

It may involve people influencing peers and superiors as well as subordinates. It can occur in the day-to-day acts of ordinary people, but it is not in any way ordinary or common.[7] Transformational leadership can exist on the micro-level of an organization where influence is a process between individuals. Transformational leadership also takes place on a macro-level, where organizations can impact social systems and institutions.

Transformational leaders are defined primarily in terms of the leader's effect on the followers.

> The dynamics of transformational leadership involve strong personal identification with the leader, joining a shared vision of the future ... going beyond the self interested exchange of rewards for mere compliance.... The transformational leader motivates followers to do more than originally expected.[8]

---

[5] Ibid., 45.

[6] G. Yukl, *Leadership in Organizations:* 3rd ed. (Englewood Cliffs, NJ: Prentice Hall, 1994).

[7] Ibid., 210.

[8] J. J. Hatter and B. M. Bass, "Superiors' Evaluation and Subordinates Perceptions of Transformational and Transactional Leadership," *Journal of Applied Psychology* 73 (1998): 695-702.

Contrasted to this transformational leadership is the "transactional" style of leadership. Whereas the transformation style of leadership is one that capitalizes on shared values, transactional leadership is based on exchange concerning things that are valued. The leader exchanges with the members of the organization something the members value. Transactional leadership is based on the self-interest of both the leaders and the followers.

> [Transactional leadership] motivates followers by appealing to their self-interest [and it] is ultimately based on self interest . . . . Transactional leadership involves values, but they are values relevant to the exchange process . . . .[9]

In a study performed in the mid 1990s, it was demonstrated that in organizations where leaders utilized a transactional style of leadership, there is generally a higher rate of employee dismissal. That is, a level of dissatisfaction occurs which either will not be or cannot be resolved through that existing style of leadership. Transformational leadership is more beneficial for the organization and the persons involved.

Educators or businessmen who employ transformational leadership would not allow merely for an exchange of services in which the school is able to function efficiently, or the shop to run smoothly, as would administrators who employ transactional leadership. The transformational style of leadership appeals to higher and nobler values; whereas, the transactional style of leadership employs values that are tangible and negotiable. However, the two styles are not unrelated.[10] Transactional leadership does involve values, but the values are relevant to an exchange process. I give so that you may give. It is a sort of utilitarianism that, at its best, should treat people and communities benignly so long as they are producing and focusing on the transaction.

Some researchers believe that transactional leadership cannot offer permanent and effective change, but that transformational leadership should be the dominant theme in an organization. Usually, most efforts to restructure administration have only attempted to

---

[9] Yukl, *Leadership in Organizations.*

[10] J. J. Hatter and B. M. Bass, "Superiors' Evaluation and Subordinates Perceptions of Transformational and Transactional Leadership," *Journal of Applied Psychology* 73 (1998): 695-702.

redefine the power structures that already exist within the organization. Establishing the transformational leadership style is a move to coordinate new and innovative strategies, not simply to realign existing power relationships, but to support the mission of the organization. Strong transformational leadership is a characteristic of an effective organization and an effective leader.

Interestingly, there is evidence to support a correlation between the number of years one serves as an administrator and the administrator's perception of himself or herself as a transformational leader. The longer one serves as an administrator, the more likely one perceives oneself as a transformational leader.[11]

DIMENSIONS OF TRANSFORMATIONAL LEADERSHIP

There are certain identifiable marks of a transformational leader. First, this individual identifies and articulates to the members of the community a vision aimed at enhancing the mission. Read Saint Paul's letter to the Romans:

> For I am not ashamed of the Gospel. It is the power of God for the salvation of everyone who believes: for Jew first, and then Greek. For in it is revealed the righteousness of God from faith to faith; as it is written, "The one who is righteous by faith will live" (Rom 1:16-17).

Paul does not engage in some kind of explanatory self-reproach about this task given to him by Christ. Instead, he states quite plainly that the Gospel is the source of salvation—for all. Paul's vision of his mission is an articulation of his belief in his vocation. He is trying to engage the people to whom he writes with an understanding of his mission.

Second, the transformational leader fosters and promotes collaboration. In his first letter to the Corinthians, Paul works at this

---

[11] A. M. Armocida, *Perceptions of Transformational Leadership: A Study of High School Principals,* Abstract from ProQuest File: Dissertation Abstracts Item: 9409478 (1994).

sort of collaboration. In the first letter to the Corinthians Saint Paul attempts to establish this shared vision.

> I am writing you this not to shame you, but to admonish you as my beloved children. Even if you should have countless guides to Christ, yet you do not have many fathers, for I became your father in Christ Jesus through the Gospel. Therefore, I urge you, be imitators of me. For this reason I am sending you Timothy, who is my beloved and faithful son in the Lord; he will remind you of my ways in Christ (Jesus), just as I teach them everywhere in every church (1 Cor 4:14-17).

Third, the transformational leader conveys to the members of the community an expectation for high-quality performance in their work. By communicating an expectation of excellence, the leader himself is to be an appropriate model. After all, the most influential teacher is more often than not the best witness.

Fourth, the transformational leader employs intellectual stimulation, which acts as a challenge to the members of the community to evaluate their own performance. Finally, the transformational leader is to provide individual support and respect for the members of the community.

Among these five behaviors, the most important, most influential and strongest to emerge are vision-building and fostering group goals. Less influential, but still a significant influence on transformational leadership, are individualized support and intellectual stimulation.

To sum up: A trait-based theory of leadership holds that certain personality types are destined to be leaders. A situational leadership asserts that, as the name implies, the situation in which a person finds himself in history determines the emergence of leaders. Transactional leadership is based on the exchange of something that is valued. Transformational leadership is based on appealing to noble ideals that followers can embrace and use to frame their lives, and work for the organization in such a way as to be an influence on others in the community—both as leaders and peers.

TRANSFORMATIONAL LEADERSHIP AS MORAL LEADERSHIP

We now come to another type of leadership that will, I believe, provide a segue for the type of leadership a priest exercises. In the early 1990s, an insistent voice for what is called moral leadership in organizations began to emerge. You can already see how challenging this type of leadership is in a culture such as ours in early twenty-first century North America. A call for moral leadership cannot be very welcomed in the school house, academy or industry in an age marked by relativism and a sort of ego-centrism, which allows for everything from instantaneous material self-gratification to exploiting workers, their pensions, and natural resources. However, writers in the field of organizational theory and organizational culture recognize that moral leadership is not removed from or inconsistent with transformational leadership style (or "transformative," as it is also sometimes called). Many believe that transformational leadership carries with it recognized moral implications. Thomas Sergiovanni, a noted writer in the field, makes bold the connection among transformational leadership and the moral aspects of being a leader in an organization.

> Transformative leadership ultimately becomes *moral,** in that it raises the level of human conduct and ethical aspirations of both the leader and the follower, thus transforming both. When this occurs, transformative leadership takes the form of *leadership as bonding.* The focus is on arousing an awareness that elevates goals and purposes to the level of a shared covenant. This covenant, in turn, bonds together leader and followers in a moral commitment. Leadership as bonding responds to such human needs as the desire for purpose, meaning and significance in what one does. Selfishness is replaced by selflessness, and self-interests are transcended in service to teaching and learning, not to protecting turf.[12] (*Italics are Sergiovanni's.)

Listen to the language that this author uses. The spiritual quality of the description that Sergiovanni offers is evident from a reading

---

[12] Thomas Sergiovanni, "Organizations or Communities? Changing the Metaphor Changes the Theory," *Educational Administration Quarterly* 30 (1994): 214-226.

of that passage. The terms "moral," "ethical aspirations," "bonding," "shared covenant," "moral commitment," "the desire for purpose," "meaning and significance," "selflessness," and "service," all possess a quality that is essentially different from the ideas found in the call to provide leadership based on transacted values, or even worse for the priest, leadership based on "professionalism"—a word on professionalism in a minute.

Moral leadership emerged in the field of organizational theory, and you can find evidence of it in business and educational circles. It would seem to be a sure fit to the leadership that a priest is to exercise—and it is. However, priestly leadership is more than that which is exercised in the educational or in the business world.

A WORD ABOUT PROFESSIONALISM

By "professionalism," one might mean a sort of glitzy attractive package of a priest who is quick-witted and savvy, perhaps one who sees religion as a business—how many times have you heard that? (Not unlike J. F. Power's protagonist, Father Urban, in his comic masterpiece *Mort D'Urban*.) This "professionalism" has the priest as more PR man than preacher—sort of a modernized Catholic version of Elmer Gantry, but this falls far from the ideal. People who wish for this type of professional are, I suspect, the same ones who want to do away with courses on Metaphysics and Christology, and replace them with Accounting 101 and a course on how to manage a Hedge Fund—whatever that is. The effort to assure that a priest is a professional carries with it certain positive aspects, but within it is also a danger of reductionism.

If, on the other hand, by professionalism one means the ability to deal with people, conduct parish meetings, act as a public figure, be aware of one's comportment, especially their manner of dressing and speaking, that is all well and good. The images Sergiovanni uses about leadership do not abrogate the necessity of professionalism. Many aspects of professionalism are contained within transformational leadership, as are the characteristics of a gentleman, a Christian, and I would assert, a priest—who moves beyond mere professionalism to a leadership that is distinct in its action and effect.

PROPHETIC LEADERSHIP

The priest as Moral Leader, even professional, is contained within the next model of leadership. It is to the prophet and prophetic leadership that I now turn. Author Robert Greenleaf, credited with creating a model of leadership that became known as "The Servant Leader," curiously begins his work by discussing the concept of prophecy. I say curiously, because his ideas on Servant Leadership originated within the company for which he worked—American Telephone and Telegraph—an organization rarely marked by a prophetic spirit. At that time, AT&T was among the largest employers in the world.

I will point out two things. Notice immediately that the situation and the genesis of the model take place in a purely secular setting. Yet, the model immediately employs religious language. It appears that leadership, theoretical or otherwise, cannot be removed from the world of the Spirit. This is where the priest has an advantage.

Greenleaf makes two initial points, one of which, I believe, is correct. He writes:

> I now embrace the theory of prophecy, which holds that prophetic voices of great clarity, and with a quality of insight equal to that of any age, are speaking cogently all the time. Men and women of a stature equal to the greatest of the past are with us now addressing the problems of the day and pointing to a better way ... to live fully and serenely in these times.[13]

That is, I offer, the correct part. This is entirely consistent with a Catholic understanding of prophets and prophecy. These people speak on behalf of another—as the word means. The "Other" for whom the prophet speaks is God. Prophecy and prophetic vision is contained in Sacred Scripture and by extension exists in every age. Was not Pope John Paul II prophetic? Blessed Teresa of Calcutta? Can we recognize prophetic qualities in Dorothy Day, Thomas Merton, Francis of Assisi and a host of others in the Catholic tradition? Among the qualities that are associated with a servant leader are listening, initiative, confidence, empathy, foresight and persuasion.

---

[13] Robert K. Greenleaf, *Servant Leadership: A Journey into the Nature of Legitimate Power and Greatness* (New York: Paulist Press, 1991).

In the context by which Saint Paul is telling the people of the Church in Philipi to follow his example, Paul speaks of the qualities he wants them to possess:

> Finally, brothers, whatever is true, whatever is honorable, whatever is just, whatever is pure, whatever is lovely, whatever is gracious, if there is any excellence and if there is anything worthy of praise, think about these things. Keep on doing what you have learned and received and heard and seen in me. Then the God of peace will be with you (Phil 4:8-9).

It seems a daunting task that would allow one to think he possesses all these abilities and thus establishes himself as a servant leader. But it is not a matter of operating in a manner that engages all these abilities. It is important to know when a specific ability is important. To illustrate this, I point to a phenomenon that caught the attention of psychologists in the last twenty-five years or so: Efficacy, or more specifically, self-efficacy.[14] A simplified articulation of this is that self-efficacy is a psychological construct which holds that a person is more likely to perform a task successfully if he believes himself capable of performing the task. The old adage "Nothing succeeds like success" is evidently true. A sense of self-efficacy enables a person to engage in activities in which they may not necessarily have engaged before, but believe himself capable of performing. A moral leader is not one who successfully performed every task given to him, but at the very foundation of his leadership believes himself capable of it.

Next, Greenleaf asserts, I believe incorrectly, that the reason prophets "fail" is due to the response they receive. Greenleaf writes, "Prophets grow in stature as people respond to the message. If their early attempts are ignored or spurned, their talent may wither away. It is seekers, then who make prophets . . ." If the work or ministry of a prophet depends on the manner in which his words are received, we could count just about every one of the Biblical prophets as abject failures. Many died as a result of persecution and rejection. Most preached a message that was unwelcome to a people who were unwilling to listen. The lack of a response cannot be the foundation upon which prophetic leadership is built. This is not to say that we

---

[14] Albert Bandura, *Social Foundations of Thought and Action: A Social Cognitive Theory* (New Jersey: Prentice-Hall, 1986).

do not look for success in numbers. As a prophetic leader, success must be measured in ways that move beyond mere numbers—as important as they are.

The priest as servant leader must incorporate, actually incarnate, those aspects of prophetic leadership that are recognizable in Biblical leaders. What are those characteristics? The office of prophet was due to a direct call from God. It was not the result of heredity; thus, the calling placed the prophet as subject entirely to the divine will. The prophets preserved and developed revealed religion, denounced idolatry, defended the moral law, gave counsel in political matters, and often also in matters of private life.[15] These tasks are not removed from the work of a parish priest. As a servant leader he attempts to live his life in a manner similar to the prophets of Sacred Scripture. This does not mean that he assumes the confrontational posture of a Nathan accusing David of sinfulness, or of Jeremiah telling King Zedikiah that he was to be captured by the Babylonians and enslaved if he did not follow God's commands (Jer 34:1-32). A prophet is also called to uplift a fallen people, as Isaiah does when he speaks of the liberation and forgiveness that is Israel's simply because the Lord loves them.

A prophet is also marked by an ability to offer assurance to his people that they have ultimate victory in their Lord. Micah, who often begins his prophecies with denunciations, usually ends with a statement of hope and fulfillment. Even Malachi contains passages of uncharacteristic hope and optimism. In order to be a servant leader and wear the mantle of prophet, the priest must be able to recognize the need to vary his approach to his tasks. The admonition is more than insightful: In difficult things—freedom. In easy things—strictness. In all things—charity.

Within the prophetic character, a priest must heed one of the essential aspects of a Biblical prophet. That is obedience. On the day of his ordination the priest promises both obedience and respect to his Ordinary. Not only does he make this promise to the man who ordained him but also to his successors. This act of faith, I often think, goes largely unnoticed—perhaps by all except the ordinand.

---

[15] Cf. *New American Bible*, "The Prophetic Books," United States Conference of Catholic Bishops, accessed March 14, 2010, http://www.usccb.org/nab/bible/prophetic.htm.

What it entails is a deep aspect of the mystery to which he committed himself. The respect and obedience that the man promises is not limited to going to the place assigned him. As a matter of fact, the obedience in a prophetic manner involves not only submission of one's will, but also the willingness to actualize the mission of the Church in the time, place, and manner that is offered in his many assignments. It is a matter of human nature that, caught up in the daily activities and the busyness of a priest's life, he may forget that the obedience required is not meant for the mere efficiency of a large organization, such as a diocese, archdiocese, or a religious community. The obedience of a prophet and a priest entails faithfully fulfilling the mission entrusted to him. For some priests this is a struggle when those daily activities, or even opposition to the mission, prove an obstacle too difficult to surmount. In his novel *The Power and the Glory*, Graham Greene created a priest torn between obedience to his duty, at the cost of his life, and failing in his mission by fleeing from it.

The protagonist, who goes unnamed throughout the novel and known simply as the whiskey priest, must contend with the darkness of his own sins and weak human nature as well as the oppressive government, which seeks his life. At the end of the story, the priest is captured and faces death. He wakes on the morning of the execution and is overcome with a terrible sadness.

> He felt only an immense disappointment because he had to go to God empty-handed, with nothing done at all. It seemed to him at that moment, that it could have been quite easy to be a saint. It would only have needed a little self-restraint and a little courage. He felt like someone who has missed happiness by seconds at an appointed place. He knew now that at the end there was only one thing that counted—to be a saint.[16]

The whiskey priest's sanctity was worked out in doing his duty, in staying behind when all others had fled. The saddest thing about the novel is that the reader gets the distinct impression that the whiskey priest did not understand that. He was, for whatever reason, unable to recognize that he shared in the power and glory.

---

[16] Graham Greene, *The Power and the Glory* (New York: Viking Penguin, 1990), 277-278.

Not all priests are able to live the gift of priesthood in such an extraordinary setting. If we examine the leadership role of a priest, we see implications for the way he spends his day. It is not only the many situations in which a priest is to manifest leadership; it is also a matter of effectiveness for a vast variety of demands. Of three or four days in a parish, a priest certainly can be counted on to take a leadership role in any—or more likely all—of a variety of tasks. What are those things and in what situations is a priest to act as a prophetic leader? I recently spoke to a priest ordained only a short while ago. He is assigned to a parish with part-time work in a high school. I called him and simply asked, "Tell me what you have done since Sunday." His response included the following.

Celebrated two Masses on Sunday and Mass each day
Anointed a parishioner between Masses
Celebrated Baptisms
Con-validation of a marriage
Met with the parish youth group
Attended a staff meeting
Had an appointment with computer technicians to re-network office space
Met with a couple seeking an annulment
Met with couples seeking con-validation for their marriage
Attended to duties at the high school
Celebrated Mass at the school
Spoke with local pastors of students who attend the school
Held Penance services from 11:30 to 2:30 at the high school
Returned phone calls
Attended a parish Penance service in another parish
Visited parochial school
Celebrated the nursing home Mass
Met with children who needed the sacrament of Confirmation
Held a wedding rehearsal
Taught RCIA
Celebrated Benediction
Met with family of a deceased parishioner to discuss funeral arrangements

I called on a Wednesday morning so that list represents only three days of the week. It seems that a priest's leadership is not only about transformation; it is about stamina.

In each of those situations, a priest is simply performing the tasks which are an aspect of an ordinary day. The opportunity for leadership and holiness in priestly service occurs most frequently in the setting which we most often occupy. In *Presbyterorum Ordinis,* the Fathers of the Second Vatican Council wrote:

> Among the virtues that priests must possess for their sacred ministry, none is so important as a frame of mind and soul whereby they are always ready to know and do the will of him who sent them, and not their own will. The divine task that they are called by the Holy Spirit to fulfill surpasses all human wisdom and human ability. "God chooses the weak things of the world to confound the strong" (1 Cor 1:27). Aware of his own weakness, the true minister of Christ works in humility trying to do what is pleasing to God. Filled with the Holy Spirit, he is guided by him who desires the salvation of all men. He understands this desire of God and follows it in the ordinary circumstances of his everyday life. With humble disposition, he waits upon all whom God has sent him to serve in the work assigned to him and in the multiple experiences of his life.[17]

The priest's leadership as a prophet, not unlike Biblical prophets, places him in a unique relationship with the people "whom God has sent him to serve ..."

JESUS THE LORD: TEACHING ON LEADERSHIP

Jesus' teaching on leadership is both prophetic and servant-based. Recall the passages in the Gospels in which Jesus instructs the Twelve on the meaning of His leadership. These passages usually come within the context of a member of the College of the Apostles seeking their own position. What is particularly shocking, if not horrifying, is

---

[17] Second Vatican Council, *Presbyterorum Ordinis,* no. 15.

the request for advancement comes upon the heels of Jesus speaking about His own upcoming suffering and death. Their request for advancement presents the reader with a new level of insensitivity.

Jesus takes to Himself the role of servant and admonishes His disciples to do the same:

> ... whoever wishes to be great among you shall be your servant; whoever wishes to be first among you shall be your slave. Just so, the Son of Man did not come to be served but to serve and to give his life as a ransom for many (Mt 20:26-28).

The reference to servant-hood in the Gospels occurs in the context of a prediction of the suffering. This is true of the synoptic accounts and the Gospel of John. John also associated the model of servant leader within the Lord's Supper, at which Jesus washes the feet of the twelve—perhaps among the greatest symbols of what it means to be a servant leader.

> ... during supper, fully aware that the Father had put everything into his power and that he had come from God and was returning to God, he rose from supper and took off his outer garments. He took a towel and tied it around his waist. Then he poured water into a basin and began to wash the disciples' feet and dry them with the towel around his waist (Jn 13:2-5).

This prophetic action of a servant leader has a profound impact on us if we realize the extent of its meaning. This task of washing the feet of guests was usually reserved for the children of the servants. In taking the role of servant to Himself, Jesus is assuming the lowest role possible. The great irony is that He is Master and Teacher, and yet performs this action—not one of humiliation but one of penetrating significance. He took on the role of servant and gave the greatest service possible: not merely washing their feet but giving of Himself.

Later in the passage Jesus raises the status of His immediate band of twelve from servant to friend. This, too, can be seen as part of the transformational style of leadership. People who engage in that style of leadership fashion a relationship with peers and subordinates in a manner consistent with their mission. In John chapter 15, we read:

> I no longer call you slaves, because a slave does not know what his master is doing. I have called you friends, because I have told you everything I have heard from my Father. It was not you who chose me, but I who chose you and appointed you to go and bear fruit that will remain, so that whatever you ask the Father in my name he may give you. This I command you: love one another (Jn 15:15-17).

The priest shares and is called to exercise, as he is able, the three-fold Episcopal tasks to teach, to lead and to sanctify. The Fathers of Vatican Council II expressed this in *Lumen Gentium* when they wrote:

> Priests, although they do not possess the highest degree of the priesthood, and although they are dependent on the bishops in the exercise of their power, nevertheless they are united with the bishops in sacerdotal dignity. By the power of the sacrament of Orders, in the image of Christ the eternal high Priest, they are consecrated to preach the Gospel and shepherd the faithful and to celebrate divine worship, so that they are true priests of the New Testament. Partakers of the function of Christ the sole Mediator, on their level of ministry, they announce the divine word to all. They exercise their sacred function especially in the Eucharistic worship or the celebration of the Mass by which acting in the person of Christ and proclaiming His Mystery they unite the prayers of the faithful with the sacrifice of their Head ... [18]

These activities are not only compatible but appear to be cor-related to the characteristics of a prophet mentioned earlier. Their tasks are to preach the Gospel, to shepherd the faithful, to celebrate divine worship, and unite the people to the Lord. These tasks do not reduce the priest to a functionary, nor do they elevate him to a status removed from or above the situation in which he finds himself. These tasks actually root him, bind him, tie him to the reality that he

---

[18] Second Vatican Council, *Lumen Gentium*, no. 28.

received in priestly ordination and works, with God's grace, to fulfill by the manner in which he lives his life.

The prophetic stance that a priest embraces is incomplete unless he follows the teaching of the Master on the issue of leadership. For a priest, that is worked out and acquired over time and in the manner that he is able, through his own abilities and responding to the grace of God offered to him. He can become an instrument of transformation for the people he serves and for himself and his own salvation. While there are those exceptional moments and events to which a priest is present—simply because he is a priest—his ministry is lived through the faith-filled words and works he is charged to speak and live on a daily basis. This is done, not usually in dramatic moments, but in the regular, daily, sometimes challenging—sometimes ordinary way in which he lives the vocation he was blessed to receive. As the Biblical prophets who serve as a model, and above all in imitation of the Master, the priest lives as servant.

To close, a last excerpt from the *Decree on the Ministry and Life of Priests*.

> Hence, those who exercise the ministry of the spirit and of justice will be confirmed in the life of the spirit, so long as they are open to the Spirit of Christ, who gives them life and direction. By the sacred actions which are theirs daily as well as by their entire ministry which they share with the bishop and their fellow priests, they are directed to perfection in their lives. Holiness does much for priests in carrying on a fruitful ministry. Although divine grace could use unworthy ministers to effect the work of salvation, yet for the most part God chooses, to show forth his wonders, those who are more open to the power and direction of the Holy Spirit, and who can by reason of their close union with Christ and their holiness of life say with Saint Paul: "yet I live, no longer I, but Christ lives in me" (Gal 2:20).[19]

---

[19] Cf. also Second Vatican Council, *Presbyterorum Ordinis*, no. 12.

REFLECTION QUESTIONS

1. There were various qualities of leadership throughout history. Certain disciplines or activities value some personal characters rather than others. What personal characteristics should be recognizable in a priest when he acts as leader?

2. Situational leadership is a recognized phenomenon in research and practice. Identify situations in which a priest is called on to be a leader and discuss the ways in which he can both share the leadership role and empower others to act as leaders.

3. Transformational leadership allows for change to take place on a personal and community level. In what ways is a priest able to act as a transformational leader?

4. Transactional leadership is a valid form of leadership but can be less desirable in a parish setting in which a priest provides leadership. What are some identifiable limits that would necessarily emerge if a priest were to act as a transactional leader in a parish?

5. It is not uncommon for people to attempt to place a business or corporate model of leadership on a priest. If this is done and a priest accepts this model of leadership, what would be the potential benefit and what are the potential costs?

6. An emerging framework for leadership in education that came about in the last two decades calls on educational leaders to be "Moral Leaders." This would seem to be a natural fit for a priest to adapt to himself. Identify three ordinary activities of a priest and discuss how he can act as a moral leader in those activities.

7. Prophetic leadership often comes with a cost. This is demonstrated in Sacred Scripture. What risks would a priest assume to himself if he lives and works as a leader in a prophet mode?

SUGGESTED READINGS

Burns, J. M. *Leadership*. New York: Harper and Row, 1978.

Dulles, Avery Robert. *The Priestly Office: A Theological Reflection*. New York: Paulist Press, 1997.

Hoge, Dean R. *The Future of Catholic Leadership: Responses to the Priest Shortage.* Kansas City, MO: Sheed & Ward, 1987.

National Conference of Catholic Bishops. *To Teach as Jesus Did.* Washington, DC: United States Catholic Conference, 1973.

John Paul II. *Gift and Mystery: On the Fiftieth Anniversary of My Priestly Ordination.* New York: Doubleday, 1996.

Palestini, Robert. *A Game Plan for Effective Leadership: Lessons from 10 Successful Coaches in Moving Theory to Practice.* Lanham, MD: Rowman & Littlefield Education, 2008.

Sergiovanni, T. J. *Moral Leadership.* San Francisco: Jossey-Bass, Inc., 1992.

Sipe, James W. *Seven Pillars of Servant Leadership: Practicing the Wisdom of Leading by Serving.* New York: Paulist Press, 2009.

Vatican Council II. *Decree on the Ministry and Life of Priests.* (*Presbyterorum Ordinis*), 1965.

Yukl, G. *Leadership in Organizations.* 3rd ed. Englewood Cliffs, NJ: Prentice Hall, 1994.

Epilogue

A PRIEST IS

Rev. Dennis J. Billy, C.Ss.R.

A priest is a man of God. He follows the way of the Lord Jesus. He lives his life for the sake of the kingdom. He sees things the way Jesus sees them. He is someone who thinks before he acts, and who prays before he thinks. He counts his words and means what he says. He speaks from the heart and puts his words into action. He is a man for others, someone who seeks to serve rather than be served. He treats everyone as a brother or a sister. He is a friend of the poor and marginalized. He extends a helping hand to them and actively seeks their well being.

A priest stands up for what is right. He speaks the truth. He exhorts others to do the same. He celebrates the sacraments with a simple dignity. He baptizes, "In the name of the Father, and of the Son and of the Holy Spirit." He is called to sacrifice and to offer sacrifice. He celebrates the Eucharist and invites others to partake of Jesus' Body and Blood. He prays for the community and on behalf of it. With his arms extended in prayer, he embraces both the whole world and his small part of it. He gives witness to Christ in both life and death. He sees beyond the present dimensions of time and space. He yearns for the coming of the kingdom, and looks for it both within his heart and in his midst.

A priest celebrates life. He also celebrates death. He senses death in the midst of life, and life in the midst of death. He helps others both to celebrate life and to mourn its passing. He helps others to grieve the loss of those they love and to live in hope of one day seeing them again. He knows when to listen, when to offer a word of comfort, and when simply to sit in silence. He is not afraid to bow his head, to shed a tear, or to hold somebody's hand in prayer. Nor is he afraid to smile, to laugh, or to lighten people's hearts. He believes that love is stronger than death, and that love is the only reason worth living. He is a man of faith, a man of hope, a man of love, a man of joy.

A priest is human. He sins. He knows what it means to be lonely. Sin and loneliness both humble and encourage him. They weigh him down, but also challenge him. They make him weak, yet also strong. They help him feel the pain of others and to suffer with them in their daily trials. They bring him to his knees, and to conversion of heart. He confesses his sins and receives God's forgiveness. He befriends his loneliness and discovers solitude of heart. He asks for forgiveness, learns to accept it, and also how to extend it to others. He befriends others, allows others to befriend him, and builds with them the family of God. He is an inviting and welcoming presence. With him, there is always an extra place at the table of the Lord.

A priest is a man of the people. He comes from them and goes back to them. He listens to their stories. He ponders them. He helps them find their voice. He helps them discover meaning in their lives by showing them how to recognize the hand of God in all that happens. He journeys with them through life, reminding them of both their origins and destiny in God. He teaches them both how to pray and how to listen. He shares his life with them and allows them to share their lives with him. He makes himself a part of their story and invites them to become a part of his. He enjoys the company of others. He recognizes their gifts and encourages them to be used in service to others. He lives to serve others and to offer his life on their behalf.

A priest is a man of God. He is a father, a teacher, a healer, and a leader. He uses his talents for the sake of others. He draws attention not to himself, but to God. He is an apostle, a disciple, a follower of Christ. The Cross is his symbol; the empty tomb, his hope; the Church, his home; the people of God, his family. He is the salt of the earth. He gives flavor to people's lives and taste to the moments that fill it. He is both *their* friend and *God's* friend. He lives the Gospel and is willing to die for it. For him, there is only Christ. Nothing else matters. Nothing else concerns him. He is a priest, a man of God, a friend of the poor, a person to trust and to count on, another Christ. He yearns to love and to be loved. He is willing to lay down his life for his friends. He is a priest, a man of God. He follows the way of the Lord Jesus.

LIST OF CONTRIBUTORS

Rev. Dennis J. Billy, C.Ss.R. is scholar-in-residence and holder of the John Cardinal Krol Chair of Moral Theology at St. Charles Borromeo Seminary, Overbrook.

Rev. Patrick J. Brady, S.T.D. is Professor and Chair of the Department of Sacred Scripture at St. Charles Borromeo Seminary, Overbrook.

Rev. Anthony J. Costa, S.T.D. is Spiritual Director of the College Division of St. Charles Borromeo Seminary, Overbrook.

Rev. Msgr. David E. Diamond, Ph.D. is the former Vice Rector of St. Charles Borromeo Seminary, Overbrook.

Rev. Msgr. Michael K. Magee, S.T.D. is Professor and Chair of the Systematics Department at St. Charles Borromeo Seminary, Overbrook.

Rev. Robert A. Pesarchick, S.T.D. is Professor and Academic Dean of St. Charles Borromeo Seminary, Overbrook.

Rev. Msgr. Joseph G. Prior, S.T.D. is former Rector of St. Charles Borromeo Seminary, Overbrook.

Cardinal Justin Rigali is the Archbishop of Philadelphia and Chairman of the Board of Trustees of St. Charles Borromeo Seminary, Overbrook.

INDEX

About Leonine Publishers

Leonine Publishers LLC makes fine Catholic literature available to Catholics throughout the English-speaking world. Leonine Publishers offers an innovative "hybrid" approach to book publication that helps authors as well as readers. Please visit our web site at www.leoninepublishers.com to learn more about us. Browse our online bookstore to find more solid Catholic titles to uplift, challenge, and inspire.

Our patron and namesake is Pope Leo XIII, a prudent, yet uncompromising pope during the stormy years at the close of the 19th century. Please join us as we ask his intercession for our family of readers and authors.

Do you have a book inside you? Visit our web site today. Leonine Publishers accepts manuscripts from Catholic authors like you. If your book is selected for publication, you will have an active part in the production process. This insightful book is an example of our growing selection of literature for the busy Catholic reader of the 21st century.

www.leoninepublishers.com